EUROPEAN JOURNAL OF WORK AND ORGANIZATIONAL PSYCHOLOGY

Editor
Peter Herriot (UK)
Editorial Team
René Bouwen (Belgium), John Hurley (Ireland)
José Peiró (Spain), John Toplis (UK)
Dieter Zapf (Germany)
Book Review Editor
John Hurley, Dublin Business School, Dublin City University, Dublin 9, Ireland
Professional News Editor
John Toplis, Training and Development Group, The Post Office,
49 Featherstone Street, London EC1Y 8SY, UK

European Journal of Work and Organizational Psychology is published by Psychology Press, an imprint of Erlbaum (UK) Taylor & Francis Ltd. Correspondence for the publisher should be addressed to *European Journal of Work and Organizational Psychology*, Psychology Press, 2 Park Square, Milton Park, Abingdon, Oxfordshire, OX14 4RN.

Subscription rates to Volume 5, 1996 (4 issues) are as follows:
To individuals: EC: £40.00 • North America: $72.00 • Rest of world: £45.00
To institutions: EC: £80.00 • North America: $144.00 • Rest of world: £85.00
Members of the International Association of Applied Psychology and the European Association of Work and Organizational Psychology qualify for a reduced subscription rate of £15.00.

New Subscriptions and changes of address should be sent to Psychology Press, c/o Turpin Distribution Centre, Blackhorse Road, Letchworth, Herts SG6 1HN, UK. Please send change of address notices at least six weeks in advance, and include both old and new addresses.

Advertising enquiries should be sent to the advertising sales office: REW Space Sales, 11 Bourne Way, West Ewell, Surrey KT19 9PP, UK.

European Journal of Work and Organizational Psychology is covered by the following indexing/abstracting services: Ergonomics Abstracts; Sociological Abstracts; SOPODA (Social Planning/Policy and Development Abstracts).

Typeset by the Laverham Press, Salisbury, Wilts

EUROPEAN JOURNAL OF WORK AND ORGANIZATIONAL PSYCHOLOGY, 1996, 5 (2), 161–164

Foreword

Dieter Zapf

University of Konstanz, Germany

Heinz Leymann

University of Umeå, Sweden

Practical experience tells us that conflicts at work, with sometimes rather negative consequences for the individuals concerned, appear in every firm. Severe cases of harassed, mobbed, bullied, or ganged-up upon individuals are personally known to many employees, as shown by the strong public reaction to the issue of mobbing in several European countries. Mobbing includes behaviours such as giving a person humiliating or senseless tasks to do, socially isolating a person, verbal threats, physical maltreatment, spreading rumours, or making fun of an individual's private life. Such behaviours are certainly as old as humankind. Nevertheless, mobbing was not picked up as an issue of scientific interest until the mid-1980s, with only a few exceptions (e.g. Brodsky, 1976). Leymann began to study mobbing and wrote a first research report in 1984 (Leymann & Gustavsson, 1984). A series of studies followed (see Leymann, this issue) and other research projects were started in the Northern European countries (Björkqvist, Österman, & Hjelt-Bäck, 1994; Einarsen, Raknes, Matthiesen, & Hellesöy, 1994; Vartia, 1993). Through the initiative of Leymann, the concept of mobbing became popular in the German-speaking countries, and some scientists started their own research, mainly based on Leymann's work (Knorz & Zapf, 1996; Kulla, Gundlach, & Zapf, 1996; Niedl, 1995). In April 1995, the guest editors of this issue organized a symposium on mobbing at the Seventh European Congress on Work and Organizational Psychology held in Györ, Hungary. This symposium brought most of the "mobbing researchers" together for the first time.

Mobbing, bullying, or harassment at work literature can still hardly be found in international computer databases. This is primarily due to the fact that most of the publications on mobbing are in Swedish, Norwegian,

Requests for reprints should be addressed to D. Zapf, Universität Konstanz, Sozial-wissenschaftliche Fakultät, Arbeits- & Organisationspsychologie, Post-box 5560, D42, D-78434 Konstanz, Germany. Email: Dieter.Zapf@uni-konstanz.de

Finnish, or German (a few exceptions are Björkqvist et al., 1994; Einarsen, Raknes, & Matthiesen, 1994; Leymann, 1990). Therefore, the idea was born at the conference in Hungary to publish the contributions of the symposium in English in order to make mobbing research accessible for the international public. The new concept of *The European Journal of Work and Organizational Psychology* to publish special issues directed both at scientists and practitioners offered an ideal opportunity to put this idea into practice.

A few words are needed on the terminology. In this issue Leymann discusses the origin of the term mobbing and his detailed view of how bullying and mobbing could be used. Suffice to say here, that as happens so often in the social sciences complications with terminology have arisen. Coming from different research traditions the contributors of this issue prefer to use somewhat different terms. Some use "mobbing" as suggested by Leymann (this issue), some prefer the term "bullying". Both terms do not in their original meaning perfectly match what is meant in the context of mobbing research. In addition, for some countries (such as the German-speaking ones), it is somewhat odd to first introduce the English term "mobbing" and then retranslate "mobbing" with "bullying". Because "bullying" puts the aspect of physical aggression too much in the foreground, which is certainly not the case in organizational contexts, we prefer the term "mobbing". Nevertheless, some of the other contributors use the term "bullying" instead with good reason. With regard to the meaning there are certainly no differences intended. Rather, "mobbing", "bullying", or "harassment" are used interchangeably.

In this issue we have tried to bring together the European mobbing researchers. We sought actively theoretical, empirical, and practical contributions. Mobbing is discussed within the context of stress research. Stress is an interdisciplinary concept, which is reflected by the psychological, medical, or economic backgrounds of the contributors, who are both scientists and practitioners.

Heinz Leymann starts with a contribution summarizing the main theoretical concepts of mobbing and some of the most important empirical findings of his mobbing research of the last 10 years.

Ståle Einarsen and Anders Skogstad present some epidemiological findings of bullying from a large Norwegian sample. Using a somewhat different empirical approach they come to very similar results to those of Leymann in Sweden. The authors also draw parallels to the research on bullying at school.

Maarit Vartia reports findings from a Finnish study, which suggest the importance of leadership and social climate for the occurrence of mobbing at work.

Dieter Zapf, Carmen Knorz, and Mathias Kulla investigated two samples of mobbing victims in Germany. Using factor analysis they differentiated several types of mobbing and found differences in frequency and different relationships with regard to health variables, and task-related and social factors at work.

Klaus Niedl reports results on the frequency of mobbing and effects on well-being in a sample of employees in an Austrian hospital. Based on a small exploratory study of 10 patients of a German clinic he argues that mobbing victims do not use simple fight or flight strategies. Rather they try various ways to cope with the problem. The more destructive behaviour (from the standpoint of the organization) of inner drawback (doing only what is absolutely necessary) or leaving the organization is usually only the final reaction after the failure of more constructive strategies.

Heinz Leymann and Anneli Gustafsson suggest that the so-called post-traumatic stress disorder (PTSD) is the correct diagnosis for many mobbing victims. They describe the typical symptoms of PTSD and report some results from a large field study and from 64 patients of the Swedish mobbing clinic.

Dieter Groeblinghoff and Michael Becker present two cases of mobbing victims who were mobbed by the same person. They illustrate the process of mobbing and the severeness of the resulting ill-health symptoms. They also present a concept of the clinical diagnosis and treatment of mobbing victims.

Finally, Martin Resch and Marion Schubinski summarize the practical experiences in the prevention and intervention of mobbing at work.

We hope that this special issue on "Mobbing and Victimization at Work" will help to disseminate the knowledge of mobbing and will stimulate research in different countries. These are important prerequisites to helping the victims of mobbing at work.

REFERENCES

Björkqvist, K., Österman, K., & Hjelt-Bäck, M. (1994). Aggression among university employees. *Aggressive Behavior, 20*, 173–184.

Brodsky, C.M. (1976). *The harassed worker*. Toronto: Lexington Books, DC Heath & Company.

Einarsen, S., Raknes, B.I., & Matthiesen, S.B. (1994). Bullying and harassment at work and its relationship with work environment quality: An exploratory study. *The European Work and Organizational Psychologist, 4*(4), 381–401.

Einarsen, S., Raknes, B.I., Matthiesen, S.B., & Hellesöy, O.H. (1994). *Mobbing og person-konflikter. Helsefarlig samspill på arbeidsplassen [Bullying and personified conflicts: Health-endangering interaction at work]*. Bergen, Norway: Sigma Forlag.

Knorz, C., & Zapf, D. (1996). Mobbing—eine extreme Form sozialer Stressoren am Arbeitsplatz [Mobbing—an extreme form of social stressors at work]. *Zeitschrift für Arbeits- und Organisationspsychologie, 40*, 12–21.

Kulla, M., Gundlach, G., & Zapf, D. (1996). *Die Bewältigung von Mobbing am Arbeitsplatz. Eine empirische Studie [Coping with mobbing at work: An empirical study]*. Unpublished manuscript. Universität Bielefeld, Fakultät für Psychologie und Sportwissenschaft.

Leymann, H. (1990). Mobbing and psychological terror at workplaces. *Violence and Victims,* *5*, 119–126.

Leymann, H., & Gustavsson, B. (1984). *Psykiskt våld i arbetslivet. Två explorativa under-* *sökningar [Psychological violence at work places. Two explorative studies].* Undersöknings-rapport 42. Stockholm: Arbetarskyddsstyrelsen.

Niedl, K. (1995). *Mobbing/bullying am Arbeitsplatz [Mobbing/bullying at work].* München: Rainer Hampp Verlag.

Vartia, M. (1993). Psychological harassment (bullying, mobbing) at work. In K. Kauppinen-Toropainen (Ed.), *OECD Panel group on women, work, and health* (pp. 149–152). Helsinki: Ministry of Social Affairs and Health.

EUROPEAN JOURNAL OF WORK AND ORGANIZATIONAL PSYCHOLOGY, 1996, 5 (2), 165–184

The Content and Development of Mobbing at Work

Heinz Leymann

University of Umeå, Sweden

In this article the concept of mobbing is introduced. Mobbing means harassing, ganging up on someone, or psychologically terrorizing others at work. Although mobbing is a very old phenomenon, it was not described and systematically researched until the early 1980s. The article begins with a case example, some historical notes, and a definition of mobbing, and then regards mobbing in the context of medical and psychological stress research. Several stages in the development of mobbing are described, based on about 800 case studies. Some epidemiological findings from a representative sample of the Swedish work population are reported. Causes and consequences of mobbing are discussed, and conclusions for prevention and intervention are drawn.

INTRODUCTION

Through their national work environmental legislation, Sweden, Finland, and Norway support the rights of workers to remain both physically and mentally healthy at work. Yet, in recent years, a workplace-related psychological problem has been discovered, the existence and extent of which was not known earlier. This phenomenon has been referred to as "mobbing", "ganging up on someone", "bullying", or "psychological terror". In this type of conflict, the victim is subjected to a systematic, stigmatizing process and encroachment of his or her civil rights. If it lasts for years, it may ultimately lead to expulsion from the labour market when the individual in question is unable to find employment due to the psychological damage incurred.

In this article, I will introduce this phenomenon, which certainly is very old, and is well known in every culture. Nevertheless, it was not systematically described until our research in 1982, which led to a small scientific report written in the autumn of 1983 and published in early 1984 by the National Board of Occupational Safety and Health in Stockholm, Sweden (Leymann & Gustavsson, 1984). The present article begins with a case description, followed by some historical notes, a definition of this workplace-related

Requests for reprints should be addressed to H. Leymann, Bastionsgatan 23, S-371 32 Karlskrona, Sweden.

problem, its aetiology and epidemiology. A further section will focus on both the consequences and sources of this destructive communicative behaviour. After this is a discussion of the different measures that are required during the disastrous course of the process. The article ends with some references to ongoing research around the world.

A CASE EXAMPLE

The case of Eve: A canteen supervisor at a large prison retired and a successor was needed. The employer and the personnel department were of the same opinion, that the opportunity should be used to bring about certain changes. The canteen needed to economize and at the same time offer healthier food. An individual with suitable training was found. She was employed and assigned to the kitchen where six female cooks—who all knew how to prepare a thick cream sauce but knew nothing about the impending changes—were standing in front of their ovens.

An inevitable conflict soon broke out. How was the new manager in the kitchen going to pursue the desired changes without the support of her employer? Nobody had informed the cooks of any planned change. The new methods for preparing food were totally alien to them. The idea of making provision for a relevant training course had never dawned on the employer. The cooks believed that all these new ideas came personally from Eve, their new supervisor. This caused them to turn against her. They started to gossip and counteract her instructions. Even the fact that she had a mentally handicapped child was held against her, as if her own character were responsible for this. There were continuous heated discussions. The cooks did not listen to Eve and ignored her delegation of tasks, regularly doing things that led to differences of opinion. It was maintained that Eve went far beyond the scope of her responsibility, which in fact was not true.

On a number of occasions, Eve tried to obtain descriptions of her responsibilities from the prison authorities. Top management refused her requests. Her continual requests were interpreted as insubordination. Here we should bear in mind that such job descriptions are in fact a method through which top management can express its leadership at all levels; by defining institutional hierarchy at a central level, and defining various areas of competence, an employer is provided with an indispensable control mechanism through which the various areas of responsibility can be effected. In Eve's case, the only thing that happened was that top management felt attacked by her requests and defended themselves. This legitimized the cooks' harassment of Eve as they interpreted the situation as if the top management were "on their side". The harassment continued and developed into a mobbing process, through which Eve eventually lost her authority completely. Harsh arguments took place on a daily basis. One of the top managers who accidentally overheard such an argument summoned Eve for a report. She noticed, as she entered the meeting room, that she was standing in front of some kind of court, she was given no chance to explain the situation but was heavily criticized. Top management ordered (!!) her to take sick leave, which the prison's own physician validated (!!). After having been on sick leave for more than two years (!!), Eve eventually lost her job. She never found another job again.

Analyses of this case will be given following a more formal presentation of the mobbing phenomenon.

HISTORICAL RESEARCH AND THE TERM "MOBBING"

Mobbing is a word not previously used in this context in the English language. It was used by the late Konrad Lorenz, an ethologist, in describing animal group behaviour. He called the attacks from a group of smaller animals threatening a single larger animal "mobbing" (Lorenz, 1991). Later, a Swedish physician who happened to become interested in what children could do to each other between their class hours, borrowed this terminology from Lorenz and called the very destructive behaviour of small groups of children directed against (most often) a single child, "mobbing" (Heinemann, 1972). The present research on this type of child behaviour has been carried out over the past 20 years, one of the most prominent researchers being the Norwegian Dan Olweus (e.g. 1993).

Following this tradition, I borrowed the word mobbing in the early 1980s, when I found a similar kind of behaviour in work places. I deliberately did not choose the English term "bullying", used by English and Australian researchers (in the USA, the term "mobbing" is also used), as very much of this disastrous communication certainly does not have the characteristics of "bullying", but quite often is done in a very sensitive manner, though still with highly stigmatizing effects. The connotation of "bullying" is physical aggression and threat. In fact, bullying at school is strongly characterized by such physically aggressive acts. In contrast, physical violence is very seldom found in mobbing behaviour at work. Rather, mobbing is characterized by much more sophisticated behaviours such as, for example, socially isolating the victim. I suggest keeping the word "bullying" for activities between children and teenagers at school and reserving the word mobbing for adult behaviour. Other expressions found in the literature are "harassment" or "psychological terror".

Regarding mobbing at places of work, a publication in 1976 referred to "the harassed worker" (Brodsky, 1976). In that book, for the first time, typical cases of mobbing can be studied. Nevertheless, Brodsky was not directly interested in analysing these cases, as they were presented alongside cases of workplace accidents, physiological stress, and exhaustion caused by long work hours, monotonous work tasks, etc. This book focused on the hard life of the simple worker and his situation, nowadays investigated by stress research.

Because of its socio-medical involvement and a poor discrimination between different stress situations at work, the book, written under the influence of the social and political climate of the late 1960s and early 1970s, hardly had any influence. The Swedish research in the early 1980s came about without knowledge of Brodsky's work. The reason was instead a new work environment law in Sweden in 1976, and a national research fund offering great possibilities to enter into new research areas regarding work psychology.

DEFINITION OF MOBBING IN THE WORK PLACE

An Operational Definition

Psychological terror or mobbing in working life involves hostile and unethical communication, which is directed in a systematic way by one or a few individuals mainly towards one individual who, due to mobbing, is pushed into a helpless and defenceless position, being held there by means of continuing mobbing activities. These actions occur on a very frequent basis (statistical definition: at least once a week) and over a long period of time (statistical definition: at least six months of duration). Because of the high frequency and long duration of hostile behaviour, this maltreatment results in considerable psychological, psychosomatic, and social misery. The definition excludes temporary conflicts and focuses on a point in time where the psychosocial situation begins to result in psychiatrically or psycho-somatically pathologic conditions. In other words, the distinction between "conflict" and "mobbing" does not focus on *what* is done or *how* it is done, but on the *frequency* and *duration* of what is done. This also underlines the fact that basic research carried out in Sweden (Leymann, 1990b, 1992a, 1992b; Leymann & Tallgren, 1989) has medical research concepts to lean on. Basically, it is a line of research focusing on somatic or psychological stress: how intense does mobbing have to be in order to result in psycho-logical or psychosomatic illness? The research has mainly focused on the psychological and physical stress. The reader must keep in mind that the present article does not deal with psychological behavioural research but rather with research concerning psychological conditions, and resulting sick leaves. The scientific definition meant by the term "mobbing" thus refers to a social interaction through which one individual (seldom more) is attacked by one or more (seldom more than four) individuals almost on a daily basis and for periods of many months, bringing the person into an almost helpless position with potentially high risk of expulsion.

The Relationship of Mobbing to Stress

In regard to German psychologically oriented stress research in particular, it may be argued that mobbing can be seen as a certain extensive and dangerous kind of social stress (Knorz & Zapf, 1996; Zapf, Knorz, & Kulla, this issue). The different use of terminology in different countries is a theoretical problem. Anglo-Saxon and Scandinavian research has more intensively focused on the biological character of the stress phenomenon (e.g. Karasek & Theorell, 1990) due to the fact that this research was mainly carried out in the field of stress medicine in the USA and Sweden. Stress research in Germany was often carried out by focusing on, in part, different stress items. Still another direction in the use of the term "stress" can be observed in Australia, where the term is influenced by its clinical usage as a medical diagnosis (e.g. Toohey, 1991). These circumstances cause some confusion when comparing the results from stress research within these different research areas. Thus, discussions can arise concerning the difference between stress and mobbing (Leymann, 1993c) as the confusion about the content of the terminology does not make it clear whether mobbing is the source of stress or the result of it. We must await further results to determine what should be understood as "stress". In Scandinavian research, as in the present article, mobbing is seen as an extreme social phenomenon, triggered by extreme social stressors, causing a range of negative effects, e.g. biological and psychological stress reactions. Thus, my use of the terminology implies that stress is the term always used for the reaction to a stimulus, referred to as a stressor. The reaction is seen as always being of biological nature with psychological effects which may be responsible for changes in behaviour (how situations are appraised, how they are dealt with, etc.; see also Lazarus, 1996). Within this theory, the logical conclusion is that, for example, very poor psychosocial conditions at workplaces may result in biological stress reactions, measurable by the adrenaline production in the body. This in turn can stimulate feelings of frustration. Through psychological processes (especially if employees lack knowledge of how to analyse social stressors at work), frustrated persons can, instead, blame each other, thus becoming each other's social stressors, and triggering a mobbing situation for a single person. Mobbing is thus an extreme social stressor, bringing about stress reactions, which in their turn can become social stressors for others.

The Relationship of Mobbing to Conflict

As originally understood in the Swedish research carried out since 1982, mobbing should be viewed as an exaggerated conflict. Mobbing evolves from a conflict after a certain time, sometimes very quickly, sometimes after weeks or months, leading to the described characteristics. In social psychology, research on aggression and conflict is voluminous. Nevertheless, this phenomenon has not been detected, the reason probably being that the social context in which it develops and is carried out changes (see the section on the course of mobbing). Another probable reason is that conflict researchers have investigated many things but have never focused on the health outcomes of the persons involved in the conflict. Therefore, experiences from "conflict solving" may not necessarily be helpful (Zapf et al., this issue).

IDENTIFICATION OF MOBBING ACTIVITIES

Identification of hostile activity variables resulted in the possibility of understanding the structure of the mobbing process. It then became apparent that these activities, although they were negatively used in such cases, in themselves did not always have a purely negative character. They consisted to a great extent of quite normal interactive behaviours. However, used highly frequently and over a long period of time in order to harass, their content and meaning changed, consequently turning into dangerous, communicative weapons (see for example case studies in Leymann, 1992b and 1993b). Their systematic use in this type of interaction triggers the development of the very stereotypical course of the mobbing process.

Due to this conceptualization, a typology of activities could be developed and subdivided into five categories depending on the effects they have on the victim. The following results are from informal interviews and heuristic analyses:

1. Effects on the victims' possibilities to communicate adequately (management gives you no possibility to communicate; you are silenced; verbal attack against you regarding work tasks; verbal threats; verbal activities in order to reject you; etc.).
2. Effects on the victims' possibilities to maintain social contacts (colleagues do not talk with you any longer or you are even forbidden to do so by management; you are isolated in a room far away from others; you are "sent to Coventry"; etc.).
3. Effects on the victims' possibilities to maintain their personal reputation (gossiping about you; others ridicule you; others make fun about your handicap, your ethnical heritage, or the way you move or talk; etc.).
4. Effects on the victims' occupational situation (you are not given any work tasks at all; you are given meaningless work tasks; etc.).
5. Effects on the victims' physical health (you are given dangerous work tasks; others threaten you physically or you are attacked physically; you are sexually harassed in an active way; etc.).

In all, 45 different activities used during a mobbing process were identified (see the item lists in Leymann, 1992b and 1993b). The item list has been statistically analysed using factor analyses (Niedl, 1995; Zapf et al., this issue) leading to similar categories. It must, nevertheless, be emphasized that these activities mainly describe hostile interactions as carried out in northern European countries (Leymann, 1992a). Studies carried out in Austria (Niedl, 1995) support an earlier hypothesis that further behaviours may be used in other cultures, while some of these from the northern European culture may not be used at all. Knorz and Zapf (1996) published a number of other behaviours found in the southern part of Germany using qualitative interviews.

Eventually a questionnaire was developed and tested (LIPT-questionnaire: Leymann Inventory of Psychological Terror; Leymann, 1990a). It has been employed in all studies mentioned previously, with the exception of the Norwegian studies which used a different investigative method.

STEREOTYPIC COURSE OVER TIME

The course of mobbing changes its character over time as the social setting changes. Scandinavian, Austrian, and Finnish research thus far reveals very stereotypical courses (Leymann, e.g. 1990b).

1. *Critical incidents.* The triggering situation is most often a conflict. Mobbing can, therefore, be seen as an escalated conflict. Not much is known about what leads the development of a conflict into a mobbing situation. Hypothetically, the first mobbing phase (which, to be exact, is not yet mobbing!) may be very short, while the next phase reveals stigmatizing actions by colleagues or shop-floor management.

2. *Mobbing and stigmatizing.* Mobbing activities may contain quite a number of behaviours which, in normal interaction, are not necessarily indicative of aggression or expulsion. However, being subjected to these behaviours almost on a daily basis and for a very long time can change their context and they may be used in stigmatizing the person in question. In fact, all of the observed behaviours, regardless of their normal meaning in normal daily communication, have the common denominator of being based on the intent to "get at a person" or punish him or her. Thus, aggressive manipulation is the main characteristic of these events.

3. *Personnel management.* When management steps in, the case becomes officially "a case". Due to previous stigmatization, it is very easy to misjudge the situation as being the fault of the subjected person. Management tends to accept and take over the prejudices produced during the previous stages. This very often seems to bring about the desire to do something in order to "get rid of the evil", i.e. the victim. This most often results in serious violations of rights, as personnel management is governed by work legislation. In this phase, the victim ultimately becomes marked/stigmatized

(Jones, 1984). Because of fundamental attribution errors, colleagues and management tend to create explanations based on personal characteristics rather than on environmental factors (Jones, 1984). This may be the case particularly when management is responsible for the psychological work environment and may refuse to accept responsibility for the situation.

4. *Expulsion*. As far as the mobbing scenario at the workplace is concerned, the social effects of expelling people from working life long before retirement are well known. This situation is probably responsible for the development of serious illnesses (Groeblinghoff & Becker, this issue; Leymann, 1995c, Leymann & Gustavsson, this issue) that cause the victim to seek medical or psychological help. However, as has been argued, the victim very easily can be incorrectly diagnosed by professionals, whether by disbelief of the person's story or by not bothering to look into the triggering social events. The most incorrect diagnoses so far are paranoia, manic depression, or character disturbance.

Comments on Eve's Case

The case clearly shows the course of a mobbing process: (1) Initially, conflicts arise, which management, despite its responsibility, does not manage to resolve. (2) As the conflict extends over time and no solution is offered, the process develops, and the harassed person is almost daily forced to experience hostilities. (3) Eventually (and this may take many months or even years), management is forced to take action. At this point, management very often accepts the gossip and the complaints from (very often just a few) colleagues without questioning their truthfulness, thus condemning the harassed person to some kind of administrative punishment. Comparing case after case, this course of events is very stereotypical. (4) Due to administrative activities, individuals in question develop such a poor reputation that it is extremely difficult to remain in the labour market; if they do so, then it is only at the loss of their earlier status as they receive only very poor work tasks in the future (Leymann, 1986, 1992b).

It must be emphasized here that it is futile to discuss *who* caused the conflict or *who* is right, even if this is of practical interest. However, there is another point at stake: We are discussing a type of social and psychological assault at the workplace, which can lead to profound legal, social, economic, and psychological consequences for the individual. These consequences are so grave and out of balance that it should be made very clear that this phenomenon, despite any other areas of interest, should be seen mainly as an encroachment of civil rights. These cases show tragic fates, including loss of civil rights, that were long ago forbidden in most societies. In the highly industrialized western world, the workplace is the only remaining "battle field" where people can "kill" each other without running the risk of being taken to court. In Sweden, it has been found that approximately 10–20% of annual suicides have mobbing processes at work in the background (Leymann, 1987).

There is a further question of exceeding importance: Should conflicts at work be allowed to get out of control and escalate into a mobbing process? Such a process should be evaluated the same way as events that lead to physical injuries. After all, these are *psychological occupational injuries* with profound consequences which can lead to life-long damage. Moreover, they are also extremely expensive for the employer.

CONSEQUENCES OF MOBBING

Effects on Society

Toohey (1991) calculated some of the costs for these and other cases of stress-related illness. Australia's costs for leave due to employees being maltreated at work are dramatic. Toohey's main criticism is focused on the fact that these employees, following long periods of being subjected to very poor psychosocial work environments, eventually consulted their physicians who diagnosed "stress" (as this is usually used in this country). Toohey's criticism is that the "health industry", by using this procedure, produces a focus on "being ill', "not being well", or "not being able to take the strain of working life", instead of forcing management, as Toohey claims should be done, to carry out enquiries into the working environments which produced the illnesses. As Toohey points out, the result of this type of policy does not give management any incentive to reorganize the working procedures of their companies.

Such highly abused employees also show a tendency towards early retirement, as has been shown by Swedish public statistics. The figures for 1992 show that as much as approximately 25% of the workforce over the age of 55 retired early. Estimates made by the Social Insurance Office reached high numbers in respect to the proportion of individuals having developed illnesses from poor psychological working environments, e.g. mobbing experiences. They varied between 20% and 40% of the yearly number of early retirements caused by poor psychosocial environments. In other words, approximately every third to fifth early retiree in this age group had suffered from extensive mobbing (personal discussions with officials from the Swedish National Board of Social Insurance, 1993).

It is not surprising that the Swedish government wanted to protect their national budget from these heavy financial burdens. At the turn of the year 1993/94, the Vocational Rehabilitation Act came into effect. This law states that employers are obligated to present a vocational rehabilitation plan to the Social Insurance Office as soon as an employee has been on sick leave for one month, or six times within a 12-month period. The purpose of this enactment is to transfer costs for rehabilitation to the origin: where poor environmental conditions trigger costly consequences (AFS, 1994).

Effects on the Organization

Johanson (1987), a Swedish business economist, developed item lists in order to calculate company costs for repetitive or long-term sick leave. He found methods to compute different kinds of costs for the company and their large sums. He could also demonstrate that it was less costly for a company to offer these employees an expensive, professional vocational rehabilitation and to reorganize working environments than to deal with employees in the way that Eve was.

Extended conflicts of this kind cause further negative development, worsening the psychosocial workplace environment. As the concept of mobbing is new, research results on these effects are not yet available. Hypothetically one can imagine its consequences in the form of higher production costs, higher personnel turnover, lack of personnel motivation, and so on.

Effects on the Victim

For the individual, mobbing is highly destructive. A common question is why does the person not leave the organization. However, as a person becomes older, his or her ability to find a new job diminishes. This is probably responsible for another fact, namely that those who have developed PTSD (post-traumatic stress disorder) because of mobbing are rarely younger than 40 years of age (Leymann, 1995c; Leymann & Gustafsson, this issue). The risk that the victim's occupational position will stagnate or even worsen is elevated (this is well demonstrated in the study of Knorz & Zapf, 1996). Expulsion from employment may easily turn into a situation in which the individual in question is unable to find any job at all, which means that he or she is essentially expelled from the labour market (e.g. Grund, 1995). Seen from these perspectives, further negative effects will most likely be detected in future research.

EPIDEMIOLOGICAL FINDINGS

Thus far, the most extensive research project on mobbing has been carried out in Sweden. As results of this study have not been published in English until now, I will very shortly describe the study and present some of the important findings. A sample of about 2400 employees, representing the entire Swedish working population, were interviewed (Leymann, 1992a, 1992c, 1992d).

Frequencies

The epidemiological statistics revealed that 3.5% ($\pm 0.7\%$; $P < 0.5$) of the collective fit into the definition of mobbing as stated previously. This prevalence means that 154,000 of the working population of 4.4 million male and female employees were subjected to mobbing. An epidemiological calculation based on this study revealed an incidence rate of 120,000 individuals as "newcomers" per year. Presuming a mean duration of 30 years in the labour market, the individual risk of being subjected to mobbing is 25%, i.e. one out of every four employees entering the labour market will risk being subjected to at least one period of mobbing of at least half a year duration during his or her working career.

Gender

Men (45%) and women (55%) are subjected in roughly equal proportions, the difference not being significant. As to the question "who is mobbing whom?", the study shows that 76% of the subjected men got mobbed by other men, whereas only 3% were attacked by women; 21% of the men were subjected by both sexes. On the other hand, 40% of the subjected women were mobbed by other women, 30% were attacked by men, and another 30% by both. This should not be interpreted according to gender. The explanation as to why men mainly get mobbed by other men and women by other women should be interpreted as a structural consequence of work life, at least in Sweden, which is still divided: men mostly work together with men and women with women. Of interest is, of course, the fact that there is quite a difference in the proportion of mobbing between the sexes. Even results of other studies confirm this tendency. It could be reasoned that men do attack women in a smaller proportion, but that the males who mobbed women are those women's superiors (both men and women more often still have a male as their superior).

Age

The observed differences are not significant. The age groups 21–30 years and 31–40 years are over-represented, compared to the three groups 41–50, 51–60, and more than 60. Niedl (1995) found other proportions in an Austrian collective.

The Number of Mobbers

About one-third of the victims were attacked by only one other person. Slightly more than 40% were subjected to attacks by two to four persons. That a whole work team should harass a single person is very rare. Future research should focus on those persons who are very well aware of the ongoing mobbing but who choose not to intervene. These persons may be seen as those who hypothetically could stop the process. The results of the Swedish study shows that there may be quite a number of "bystanders".

Occupations

Even here, the results are not significant due to the fact that the number of 2400 was still not large enough for studies of subgroups. Nevertheless, tendencies show that some branches may be over-represented (in the following, the proportion of the entire workforce in a given branch is shown in brackets): 14.1% (6.5%) of the subjected persons in the study work in schools, universities, and other educational settings. A study of patients in the Swedish so-called "mobbing clinic" (Leymann, 1995c) shows an over-proportion of patients who worked in schools, universities, hospitals, child care centres, and religious organizations. About three-quarters of the patients at this hospital were women. Also these findings should not be interpreted genderwise. The explanation may be that just these work places have larger shortcomings regarding organization, work task content, and management. The reason for this, in its turn, may be organizational difficulties as these work places are controlled by more than one hierarchy, e.g. by politically chosen groups and so on. So far, this has not been studied in detail. The overproportion of women in the patient group may be caused by the fact that these work places employ women in a larger proportion than men.

Long-term Effects

A greater proportion of these subjected employees (the study points roughly towards 10–20%) seem to contract serious illnesses or commit suicide. Leyman (1987) points out that about every sixth to 15th officially noted suicide in the Swedish statistics (in all about 1800 every year) may be caused by this kind of workplace problem.

Early International Comparisons

Direct comparisons can not, so far, be done as studies from different countries are still so few. Nevertheless, a number of studies carried out at different kinds of workplace show minor differences in regard to countries and branches (Leymann, 1992e, 1992f; Leymann & Lindroth, 1993; Niedl, 1995; Paanen & Vartia, 1991). In Sweden, companies within the private sector show a slightly lower mobbing frequency compared with public service organizations where the frequency is higher. In Finland and Austria, the general frequency was higher than in Sweden. Studies pertaining to the prevalence of mobbing at Norwegian workplaces are impossible to compare due to the fact that quite a different study method was used.

WHY DOES MOBBING TAKE PLACE?

The question is, then, why mobbing processes develop in the first place. Widely spread prejudices maintain that the problem arises once an employee with character difficulties enters the workforce. The research thus far has not been able in any way to validate this hypothesis, neither with respect to mobbed employees at workplaces, nor mobbed children at schools (see the literature mentioned earlier in this article). What then does research, so far, show as its probable causes?

The Work Organization as a Factor

Analyses of approximately 800 case studies show an almost stereotypic pattern (Becker, 1995; Kihle, 1990; Leymann, 1992b; Niedl, 1995). In all these cases, extremely poorly organized production and/or working methods and an almost helpless or uninterested management were found. This is not surprising keeping in mind the mostly poor organizational conditions that Leymann (1992b, 1995c) found for mobbed employees from hospitals, schools, and religious organizations, which were over-represented in these studies.

Let us take the work organization at a hospital as observed in some of these cases as an example. Quite a few nurses whom we interviewed did not really know who their boss was. A hospital has at least two parallel hierarchies: one represented by doctors responsible for diagnosing and determining treatments, and one represented by a hierarchy of nurses responsible for carrying out the treatment. Both hierarchies have their management that gives orders and supplies bosses for the nurse, both kinds of boss have the authority to tell her what to do or what not to do. Commonly extensive workloads arise either because of a shortage in the workforce or due to poor work organization on a daily basis. Often, the unofficial institution of spontaneous leadership (marked as dangerous in the literature on management and organization) is a necessity to get things accomplished at all. This results in a situation where a nurse can occasionally take over the command within a group of nurses without having the authority to do so in order to accomplish the work. Clear-cut rules for this unofficial procedure, or knowledge of whether or not fellow colleagues will accept this, do not exist. All of these are in fact high-risk situations and can very easily result in conflicts. When this happens, whether the conflict will be prolonged or easily settled depends very often on the existing type of group dynamics and not on (as it should be) whether management has the training and motivation to solve conflicts. Especially in a working world where almost only women are employed, conflicts tend to become harsher as women are more dependent on social, supportive group dynamics (Björkqvist, Österman, & Hjelt-Bäck, 1994).

Poor Conflict Management as a Second Source

The situation gets far more dangerous if the manager of one of these hier-archies wants to be part of the social setting. If the supervisor, instead of sorting out the problem, is actively taking part, group dynamically, in the harassment, he or she also has to choose sides. As we have seen in very many cases, this stirs up the situation and makes it worse (Leymann, 1992b). In addition to this management reaction, it has been found to a high degree that when a manager simply neglects the "quarrel", the conflict is thereby given time to deepen and escalate. Poor managerial performance thus entails either (1) getting involved in the group dynamics on an equal basis and thereby heating it up further (which we have seen more often with female managers) or (2) denying that a conflict exists (which we have seen more often with male managers). Both types of behaviour are quite dangerous and are, together with poor work organization, the main causes for the development of a mobbing process at the workplace (Adams, 1992; Kihle, 1990).

Again, it must be underlined that research concerning causes of mobbing behaviour is so far still in its infancy, and in particular the difference in behaviour between male and female management is still poorly understood. Research in this area has been carried out in Finland, demonstrating that women choose mobbing activities that affect the victim more indirectly (gossip, slander, activating other individuals to carry out mobbing activities, etc.). Björkqvist, Lagerspetz, and Kaukianinen (1992) state that female aggressiveness has been widely overlooked in earlier research as variables in data collecting were oriented mainly towards male standards. According to this, Björkqvist et al. argue that this might be the reason behind the false impression that women score milder on questionnaires measuring aggres-siveness. Even here, future research will eventually focus on more causes in detail.

What About the Personality of the Victim?

As mentioned earlier, research so far has not revealed any importance of personality traits either with respect to adults at workplaces or children at school. We regard statements about character problems of single individuals by logic, as a false statement. It must not be forgotten, that the workplace should not be confused with other situations in life. A workplace is always regulated by behavioural rules. One of these rules deals with effective co-operation, controlled by the supervisor. Conflicts can always arise, but must, according to these behavioural rules, be settled. One of the super-visor's obligations is to manage this kind of situation. By neglecting this obligation (and supervisors as well as top management often do so as a consequence of shortcomings in conflict management), a supervisor promotes the escalation of the conflict in the direction of a mobbing process. Mobbing, in its early stages, is most often a sign that a conflict around the organization of work tasks has taken on a private touch. When a conflict is "privatized" or, in other words, if the power behind its further development begins to become grounded in a deeper dislike between two individuals, then the conflict concerning work tasks has become a situation that an employer has the obligation to stop. Once a conflict has reached this stage in its escalation, it is meaningless to blame someone's "personality" for it—even if (which is quite unlikely) future research should reveal personality as a source of conflicts of this kind. If a conflict has developed into a mobbing process, the responsibility lies in the first instance with the management, either due to deficient conflict management in the single situation, or due to a lack of organizational policies about handling conflict situations (Leymann, 1993b).

A further argument against the view to look at an individual's personality as a cause of mobbing processes is that when a post-traumatic stress syndrome develops, the individual can develop major personality changes as a symptom of a major mental disorder due to the mobbing process. As the symptoms of this changed personality are quite typical and distinct, it is understandable, but still false, that even psychiatrists lacking modern knowledge about PTSD as a typical victim disorder misunderstand these symptoms as being what the individual brought into the company in the first place (Leymann & Gustafsson, this issue).

MEASURES

There are a number of measures, which have been shown to be effective in these situations on a practical level, although at present there are not yet any research results available confirming these scientifically. Nevertheless, practical experiences in Sweden are numerous. Due to the fact that the National Board of Occupational Safety and Health (NBOSH) in Stockholm has distributed pedagogical material since 1989 (video, overhead, manual, books, etc.; a German translation is Leymann, 1995a and 1995b), about 300 Swedish companies have used it, according to information from NBOSH in November 1995. In fact, the educational video and further material has been a bestseller since 1989. I have myself used this material in about 100 companies. The following information is based on these practical experiences and other verbal information from the educational staff (see also Leymann, 1993a).

When to comes to selecting a measure, it is essential to know that this must be carried out according to what phase in the mobbing process is present. There are different measures available directed toward preventing its development, stopping it, or rehabilitating a subjected individual.

Precautions

It should be in the employer's interest to establish a policy in preventing conflicts from escalating into dangerous states. It seems to be nearly sufficient if the employer states that dangerous escalation of conflicts are not in the organization's interest and that top management considers prevention *by supervisors and managers* as a rule. Education of management at all levels in the art of conflict management, and training in using the policy of the company appropriately is one preventive measure. In addition, policy rules about how to act if a conflict has reached a state where conflict management becomes very demanding should exist.

Early Management Interventions

In order to intervene early, a supervisor must be capable of reading the first signs of a developing mobbing process. Top management should also appoint one or more individuals in the organization to whom employees in danger can turn to for advice. For these officials, management has to delgate authority in order to allow them to become active in the single case. Case studies thus far (Leymann, 1992b) show very clearly that inactivity at these levels also involves the supervisor being very insecure in his or her organizational role in such a conflict. A company policy should also give clear information pertaining to this. One way of early prevention and intervention is to straighten out organizational matters in the company and shape organizational order and ethics in behaviour (see the pedagogical material from the National Board of Occupational Safety and Health in Stockholm, 1989 and its German translation, Leymann, 1995a, 1995b).

Vocational Rehabilitation

As a mobbing process develops, it should be the obligation of supervisors and managers to protect the individual in danger. Stigmatization of the individual must be prevented, and he or she must be able to keep up his or her previous reputation and abilities. Should the person be urged to take sick leave, vocational rehabilitation should be offered. Present research in Sweden and Germany will reveal effective methods at a later date. However, letting an unhappy person go through a mobbing process and thereafter just dumping him or her should be classified as a major management failure.

Law

Three Scandinavian countries recognize the employee's right to remain physically *and mentally* healthy at work (Sweden, Finland, and Norway). The Swedish National Board of Occupational Safety and Health has, on top of this legislation, submitted three ordinances in order to enforce this act, one of them especially regarding mobbing. One ordinance enforces the employer to internal control of the work environment on a regular basis in order to be able to take measures at an early stage (AFS, 1992). Another ordinance enforces direct interventions as mobbing occurs at the workplace (AFS, 1993). A third ordinance in this area enforces the employer's responsibility for vocational rehabilitation once an employee has been on sick leave very often during one year or has been on sick leave for at least one month (AFS, 1994).

RESEARCH AROUND THE WORLD

This article gave an overview of the concept of mobbing, reported some epidemiological findings, and summarized various measures against mobbing. Following the publication of a first research paper (Leymann & Gustavsson, 1984) and a first book (Leymann, 1986), the concept of mobbing has been picked up in a number of different countries for further scientific development. Research so far has been carried out in Norway (Einarsen & Raknes, 1991; Kihle, 1990; Matthiesen, Raknes, & Rökkum, 1989), Finland (Björkqvist et al., 1994; Paananen & Vartia, 1991), Germany (Becker, 1993; Halama, 1995; Knorz & Zapf, 1996; Zapf et al., this issue), Austria (Niedl, 1995), Hungary (Kaucsek & Simon, 1995), and Australia (McCarthy, Sheehan, & Kearns, 1995; Toohey, 1991). Mobbing research is also about to start in the Netherlands, the UK, France, and Italy. Although some progress can be reported in this issue, it is clear that there are more open questions than empirically founded answers. It is my hope that this issue will further stimulate research in this area and make scientists and practitioners aware of the harm and suffering caused by mobbing at work.

ACKNOWLEDGEMENTS

I would like to thank Dr S. Baxter for her help with the translation and Dr J. Knispel for his research language advice (Research Language Advice, 22303 Hamburg, Mühlenkamp 8D).

REFERENCES

Adams, A. (1992). *Bullying at work*. London: Virago Press.
Arbetarskyddsstyrelsens Författnings Samling. (1992). *Internkontroll av arbetsmiljön [Internal control of work environment]* (Vol. 6). Stockholm: Arbetarskyddsstyrelsen.
Arbetarskyddsstyrelsens Författnings Samling. (1993). *Kränkande särbehandling i arbetslivet [Victimization at work]* (Vol. 17). Stockholm: Arbetarskyddsstyrelsen.
Arbetarskyddsstyrelsens Författnings Samling. (1994). *Arbetsanpassning och rehabilitering [Work assignment and vocational training]* (Vol. 1). Stockholm: Arbetarskyddsstyrelsen.

Becker, M. (1993). Mobbing—ein neues Syndrom [Mobbing—a new syndrome]. *Spektrum der Psychiatrie und Nervenheilkunde, 22,* 108–110.

Becker, M. (1995). Rückwege zum Selbstbewußtsein—Ein Beispiel für die Behandlung in der Mobbingklinik [Ways back to self-confidence—an example for the treatment in the mobbing clinic]. In H. Leymann (Ed.), *Der neue Mobbing Bericht. Erfahrungen und Initiativen—Auswege und Hilfsangebote* (pp. 124–144). Reinbek bei Hamburg: Rowohlt.

Björkqvist, K., Lagerspetz, K.M.J., & Kaukianinen, A. (1992). Do girls manipulate and boys fight? Developmental trends in regard to direct and indirect aggression. *Aggressive Behavior, 18,* 117–127.

Björkqvist, K., Österman, K., & Hjelt-Bäck, M. (1994). Aggression among university employees. *Aggressive Behavior, 20,* 173–184.

Brodsky, C.M. (1976). *The harassed worker.* Toronto: Lexington Books; DC Heath and Company.

Einarsen, S., & Raknes, B.I. (1991). *Mobbing i arbeidslivet. En undersökelse av forekomst ol helsemessige av mobbing på norske arbeidsplasser [Mobbing in worklife: A study on prevalence and health effects of mobbing in Norwegian workplaces].* Bergen: Forsknings-senter for arbeidsmiljö (FAHS).

Grund, U. (1955). Wenn die hemmschwellen sinken. Die Aufgabe der Gewerkschaft: Aufklärung und Prävention [When the thresold of scruples shrink: The task of the trade unions: Information and prevention). In H. Leymann (Ed.), *Der neue Mobbing-Bericht. Erfahrungen und Initiativen, Aufwege und Hilfsangebote* (pp. 93–107). Reinbek bei Hamburg: Rowohlt.

Halama, P. (1995). *Psychosozialer Streß durch Mobbing und Giftstoffe an Arbeitsplatz. [Psychosocial stress through mobbing and toxic substances at work places].* Unpublished manuscript. Hamburg.

Heinemann, P. (1972). *Mobbing—Gruppvåald bland barn och vuxna [Mobbing—group violence by children and adults].* Stockholm: Natur och Kultur.

Johanson, U. (1987). *Utveckla det mänskliga kapitalet [Developing the human capital].* Stockholm: SPF-Verlag.

Jones, E. (1984). *Social stigma—The psychology of marked relationships.* New York: W.H. Freeman.

Karasek, R., & Theorell, T. (1990). *Healthy work: Stress, productivity and the reconstruction of working life.* New York: Basic Books.

Kaucsek, G., & Simon, P. (1995, April). *Psychoterror and risk-management in Hungary.* Paper presented at the Seventh European Congress of Work and Organizational Psychology, Györ, Hungary.

Kihle, S. (1990). *Helsefarlige ledere og medarbeidere [When management is a health risk for subordinates].* Oslo: Hemmets bokförlag.

Knorz, C., & Zapf, D. (1996). Mobbing—eine extreme Form sozialer Stressoren am Arbeitsplatz [Mobbing—an extreme type of social stressors at the work place]. *Zeitschrift für Arbeits- & Organisationspsychologie, 40,* 12–21.

Lazarus, R.S. (1966). *Psychological stress and the coping process.* New York: McGraw-Hill.

Leyman, H. (1986). Vuxenmobbning—om psykiskt våld i arbetslivet [Mobbing—psychological violence at work places]. Lund: Studentlitteratur.

Leymann, H. (1987). Självmord till följd av förhållanden i arbetsmiljön [Suicide and conditions at the work place]. *Arbete, människa, miljö, 3,* 155–160.

Leymann. H. (1990a). *Handbok för användning av LIPT-formuläret för kartläggning av risker för psykiskt våld i arbetsmiljön [The LIPT questionnaire—a manual].* Stockholm: Violen.

Leymann, H. (1990b). Mobbing and psychological terror at workplaces. *Violence and Victims, 5,* 119–126.

Leymann, H. (1992a). *Vuxenmobbning på svenska arbetsplatser. En rikstäckande undersökning med 2.428 intervjuer [Mobbing at Swedish work places—a study of 2428 individuals: Frequencies]*. (Delrapport 1 om frekvenser.) Stockholm: Arbetarskyddsstyrelsen.

Leymann, H. (1992b). *Från mobbning till utslagning i arbetslivet [From mobbing to expulsion in work life]*. Stockholm: Publica.

Leymann, H. (1992c). *Manligt och kvinnligt vid vuxenmobbning. En rikstäckande undersökning med 2428 intervjuer [Gender and mobbing—a study of 2428 individuals]*. (Delrapport 2.) Stockholm: Arbetarskyddsstyrelsen.

Leymann, H. (1992d). *Psykiatriska hälsoproblem i samband med vuxenmobbning. En rikstäckande undersökning med 2428 intervjuer [Psychiatric problems after mobbing—a study of 2428 individuals]*. (Delrapport 3.) Stockholm: Arbetarskyddsstyrelsen.

Leymann, H. (1992e). *Oetisk kommunikation i partiarbetet [Unethical communication in political parties]*. Stockholm: Arbetarskyddsstyrelsen.

Leymann, H. (1992f). *En svag grupps psykosociala arbetsvillkor i Sverige [The psychosocial work condition of a group of handicapped workers in Sweden]*. Stockholm: Arbetarskyddsstyrelsen.

Leymann, H. (1993a). Marketing für qualifizierte Maßnahmen zum Abbau von psychischem Terror am Arbeitsplatz [Marketing of measurements against psychoterror at work places]. In H. Geißler (Ed.), *Bildungsmarketing. Band 4 Serie Betriebliche Bildung—Erfahrungen und Visionen*. Frankfurt a.M.: Peter Lang Verlag.

Leymann, H. (1993b). Mobbing. Psychoterror am Arbeitsplatz und wie man sich dagegen wehren kann [Mobbing—psychoterror at work places]. Reinbek: Rowohlt Verlag.

Leymann, H. (1993c). Ätiologie und Häufigkeit von Mobbing am Arbeitplatz—eine Übersicht über die bisherige Forschung [Etiology and frequency of mobbing at work—a research review]. *Zeitschrift für Personalforschung, 7*, 271–283.

Leymann, H. (1995a). *Mobbing und Psychoterror an Arbeitsplatz [Mobbing and psychoterror at work places]* (Videotape). Wien: Verlag des ÖGB.

Leymann, H. (1995b). *Begleitmaterial zum Mobbing-Video [Information material for the mobbing video]*. Wien: Verlag des ÖGB.

Leymann, H. (1995c). *Hur sjuk blir man av kränkande särbehandling i arbetslivet? Diagnosstatistik över posttraumatisk stress belastning (PTSD) från de första 64 patienterna hos Sveriges RehabCenter AB Violen [How ill does one become through mobbing at work?]*. Stockholm: Arbetarskyddsstyrelsen.

Leymann, H., & Gustavsson, B. (1984). *Psykiskt våld i arbetslivet. Två explorativa undersökningar [Psychological violence at work places. Two explorative studies]*. (Undersökningsrapport 42.) Stockholm: Arbetarskyddsstyrelsen.

Leymann, H., & Lindroth, S. (1993). *Vuxenmobbning mot manliga förskollärare [Mobbing of male teachers at kindergartens]*. Stockholm: Arbetarskyddsstyrelsen.

Leymann, H., & Tallgren, U. (1989). Undersökning av frekvensen vuxenmobbning inom SSAB [A study of mobbing frequencies at SSAB]. *Arbete, människa, miljö, 1*, 110–115.

Lorenz, K. (1991). *Hier bin ich—wo bist Du? Ethologie der grauganz [Here I am—where are you? The behaviour of geese]* (New edition). München: Piper.

Matthiesen, S.B., Raknes, B.I., & Rökkum, O. (1989). Mobbing på arbeidsplassen (Mobbing at work places]. *Tidskrift for Norsk Psykologforening, 26*, 761–774.

McCarthy, P., Sheehan, M., & Kearns, D. (1995). *Managerial styles and their effects on employees health and well-being*. Brisbane: School of Organisational Behaviour and Human Resource Management, Griffith University.

National Board of Occupational Safety and Health in Stockholm. (1989). *Mobbning och utslagning i arbetslivet [Mobbing and expulsion in working life]* [Video, manual, overhead transparencies, book, discussion material]. Stockholm: Author.

Niedl, K. (1995). *Mobbing/bullying an Arbeitsplatz [Mobbing/bullying at the work place]*. München: Rainer Hampp Verlag.

Olweus, D. (1993). *Bullying at school: What we know and what we can do*. Oxford: Blackwell.

Paanen, T., & Vartia, M. (1991). *Mobbing at workplaces in state government* (in Finnish). Helsinki: Finnish Work Environment Fund.

Toohey, J. (1991). *Occupational stress: Managing a metaphor*. Sydney: Macquarie University.

EUROPEAN JOURNAL OF WORK AND ORGANIZATIONAL PSYCHOLOGY, 1996, 5(2), 185–201

Bullying at Work:
Epidemiological Findings in Public
and Private Organizations

Ståle Einarsen and Anders Skogstad

Division of Work and Organizational Psychology,
Department of Psychosocial Science, University of Bergen, Norway

The aim of the study was to investigate the prevalence of bullying and harassment at work, to identify risk groups and risk organizations, and to investigate who the victims report to be their tormentors. Bullying and harassment are defined as situations where a worker or a supervisor is systematically mistreated and victimized by fellow workers or supervisors through repeated negative acts. However, to be a victim of such bullying one must also feel inferiority in defending oneself in the actual situation. Data from 14 different Norwegian surveys ($N = 7986$) are presented, encompassing a broad array of organizations and professions. The results show that bullying and harassment at work are widespread problems in Norwegian working life. As many as 8.6% of the respondents had been bullied at work during the previous six months. Organizations with many employees, male-dominated organizations, and industrial organizations had the highest prevalence of victimization. Older workers had a higher risk of victimization than younger workers. Even if men and women do not differ in prevalence of bullying, significantly more men were reported as bullies. Victims reported superiors as bullies as often as they reported colleagues as their tormentor(s).

Since the early 1970s, bully/victim problems among schoolchildren have received substantial attention in the Scandinavian countries from both the public, the government, and from researchers (Heinemann, 1972; Olweus, 1978, 1990, 1994; Roland 1989; Roland & Munthe, 1989). In research among children, bullying is seen as long-term aggression directed towards a person who is not able to defend him/herself, leading to victimization of that person (Björkqvist, Österman, & Hjelt-Bäck, 1994). During the early 1980s bullying, harassment, or mobbing was also discovered as a problem among adults within work organizations (Leymann & Gustavsson, 1984). This discovery was due to the Swedish work environment act from 1976,

Requests for reprints should be addressed to S. Einarsen, Division of Work and Organizational Psychology, Öysteingst. 1, N-5007 Bergen, Norway. Email: Stale.einarsen@psych.uib.no

supporting the rights of workers to remain both physically and mentally healthy at work (Leymann, 1990). Somewhat later work environment acts were established in Norway and Finland which prompted research on bullying at work in these countries.

Although both clinical and anecdotal accounts of bullying and harassment at work do exist (Adams, 1992; Brodsky, 1976; Kile, 1990), as well as popular focused books on interventions and prevention methods (Adams, 1992; Einarsen, Raknes, Matthiesen, & Hellesøy, 1994; Leymann, 1991, 1992; Kaye, 1994), only a few studies have as yet been published providing information on the frequency of bullying (e.g. Björkqvist, Österman, & Hjelt-Bäck, 1994; Niedl, 1995; Vartia, 1991). Therefore, research on both the frequency and the risk groups of bullying and harassment in organizations is definitely needed.

In a study among employees at a Finnish university, Björkqvist, Österman, and Hjelt-Bäck (1994) found as many as 30% of the men and 55% of the women had been exposed to some form of harassment during the last year. Thirty-two percent of the total subjects claimed that they had observed others being harassed at their workplace during this period. A Norwegian opinion poll conducted in 1987 showed that 6% of the respondents experienced some kinds of harassment at work (cf. Matthiesen, Raknes, & Rökkum, 1989). Among 99 nurses in a psychiatric ward, as many as 10% claimed that they were bullied, teased, badgered, or frozen out by one or more of their fellow workers and that this situation was a threat to their well-being at work (Matthiesen et al., 1989). Among 460 male industrial workers, 7% were on a weekly basis exposed to acts such as repeated ridicule and insulting teasing, verbal abuse, gossip, rumours spread about oneself, or the like (Einarsen & Raknes, 1995). Although such conducts were common and experienced by most organization members now and then, they had a significant and negative relationship with psychological well-being as well as overall job satisfaction when occurring consistently and systematically. Among the nurses reported above, exposure to bullying correlated significantly with burnout, psychological complaints, and somatic health complaints (Matthiesen et al., 1989). In a study among 745 Norwegian assistant nurses, 3% were being bullied at that time, while 8.4% had previous experiences as victims (Matthiesen, 1990). Leymann and Tallgren (1989), who defined bullying as the exposure to one out of 45 predefined negative acts on a weekly basis for more than six months, found that 4% of the employees of a Swedish steelmaking company were victims of such bullying at work. According to the same definition, 3.5% of the Swedish working population are victims of bullying at work (Leymann, 1992).

With the exception of the two latter studies, none of these studies used a precise and well-defined concept of bullying and harassment at work. When measuring exposure to a sociopsychological and interactional

When measuring exposure to a sociopsychological and interactional phenomenon such as work harassment, it is highly important that the respondents possess a common and precise definition. However, the method used in the latter studies estimated the frequency of bullying through a research operation without focusing on the individual's own perception and evaluation of the potentially harassing experience. According to Painter (1991), any estimation of violence at work must take subjective vulnerability and subjective evaluation into account. The aim of the present study is therefore to investigate some epidemiological aspects of victimization from bullying at work as perceived, evaluated, and reported by the victims.

In Scandinavian countries the term "mobbing" is used in referring to situations where an employee is persistently being picked on or humiliated by leaders or fellow co-workers. Although the term "mobbing" originally refers to group aggression, the Scandinavian term also includes situations where a single individual harasses another person (see also Olweus, 1990). In this article, bullying and harassment will be used interchangeably when referring to the Scandinavian concept of "mobbing" at work. The concept of "mobbing" is thoroughly presented elsewhere in this issue (see Leymann, this issue).

In the present study a person is defined as bullied if he or she is repeatedly subjected to negative acts in the workplace. However, to be a victim of such bullying one must also feel inferiority in defending oneself in the actual situation. This definition builds on research on bullying in the school playground (Olweus, 1978, 1990, 1993) and stresses that bullying and harassment imply a difference in actual or perceived power and "strength" between the persecutor and the victim. Typically, a victim of harassment and bullying is teased, badgered, and insulted and perceives that he or she has little recourse to retaliation in kind (Brodsky, 1976). This definition of bullying and harassment is not limited to a predefined set of negative acts. It covers all situations in which one or more persons over a period feel subjected to negative acts that one cannot defend oneself against. Even if a single serious episode, e.g. physical assault, may be regarded as bullying and harassment, our definition emphasizes "repeated negative acts" (Olweus, 1990). Consequently, serious conflicts between parties of "equal" strength, or isolated episodes of conflict, are not considered as bullying. Social isolation and exclusion, devaluations of one's work and efforts, and exposure to teasing, insulting remarks, and ridicule, were the most commonly experienced negative acts by 137 Norwegian victims of bullying at work who were identified by self-report according to this definition, (Einarsen, Raknes, Matthiesen, & Hellesøy, 1994). Although some victims reported undesirable sexual attention or advances, this seemed to be a minor group of negative acts.

METHOD

Research Questions

The primary aim of this study is to investigate the prevalence and demo-graphical risk groups of bullying and harassment in Norwegian working life using definitions and methods developed in research on bullying among schoolchildren. While bullying among adults is a rather new field of inquiry, substantial theoretical and methodological developments have been achieved in the field of bullying among children (see Olweus, 1993, 1994). Period prevalence rate will be used when estimating the frequency of exposure to bullying at work. This prevalence refers to the number of persons exposed to a certain problem or event, here bullying and harass-ment, within a certain period of time (Olweus, 1989). The time frame involved will be the previous six months, which is identical with the preval-ence period used in studies among children (see Olweus, 1978, 1994). The following research questions will be addressed:

1. How prevalent is exposure to bullying at work?
2. What are the duration of such bullying episodes?
3. Who are reported as the offenders of bullying at work?
4. May risk groups or risk organizations of bullying be identified?

Sample

The respondents of this study were selected from 14 different "Quality of Working Life" (QWL) surveys, conducted by the Research Centre for Occupational Health and Safety, University of Bergen, in the period from 1990 to 1994. Five of the studies were organization-wide (OW) surveys, including all employees on all organizational levels within one particular organization. These surveys were instigated by the management in co-operation with the employees' unions. Since the participation in organiza-tional environment programmes is required by Norwegian work environ-ment laws and regulations, all employees and managers were requested to participate. These studies therefore reflect each organization's total work-force.

One OW survey covered all employees of a Norwegian university, another two all employees within six different nursing homes. A fourth study was conducted among all employees of a marine engineering and maintenance workshop (named "industrial workers"). The fifth study included a home-based nursing and care-giving organization within the municipality of a major Norwegian city. The OW surveys were distributed and completed during work hours.

The other nine surveys were conducted in collaboration with different Norwegian labour unions and the Norwegian Employers' Federation (NHO) (see Table 1). In these Union surveys (US), a representative sample of the total population of members was randomly drawn. An anonymous self-administered postal questionnaire was mailed to each participant. Six of these samples represent local unions from the Norwegian west coast. In addition, two nationwide union surveys were included. One covered members of the Norwegian Psychological Union, the other was conducted among the health and social welfare managers of all Norwegian municipalities. The response rate varied substantially between the different surveys. Table 1 shows total populations, sample sizes, numbers of respondents, and the response rates of each survey.

In the total sample, 43.9% were men and 55.6% women. All age-groups between 17 and 70[1] were covered, with a mean age of 41 years (SD 11.9). While 7.5% of the respondents were aged 60 or older, 8.4% were 25 or less. As many as 82% were employed on a full-time basis. Most of the respondents were employed in public organizations (85%). While 4.6% had only

TABLE 1
Population, Sample, Number of Responses, and Response Rate in Each Subsample

Organization/Survey	Survey Type[b]	Population	Sample[a]	Number of Responses	Response Rate (%)
1. Teachers Union	US	2700	945	554	59
2. Trade and Commerce	US	2800	940	383	38
3. Clerical and Officials	US	974	470	265	56
4. Graphical Workers Union	US	800	397	159	40
5. Union of Hotel and Restaurant Workers	US	1187	490	172	35
6. Employers Federation (NHO)	US	1050	480	181	38
7. Electricians Union	US	1100	1020	480	47
8. University	OW	2480	2480	1470	59
9. Industrial Workers	OW	552	552	485	88
10. Psychologists Union	US	2500	2480	1402	57
11. Nursing Homes 1	OW	495	495	360	73
12. Nursing Homes 2	OW	450	450	341	76
13. Home-based Nursing	OW	1661	1661	1404	85
14. Health and Welfare Managers	US	395	395	344	87

[a]These numbers are corrected for questionnaires returned with "addresses unknown"; [b]US = union survey, OW = organization-wide survey.

[1]In Norway the retirement age is 67. One may nevertheless be employed full time until the age of 70.

finished junior high school, 51.4% had completed a college or university degree. The rest of the respondents (44.0%) had finished senior high school or had an undergraduate college degree. The main demographic characteristics of each sample are given in Table 2.

Measurements

The questionnaires employed in the studies included demographic variables, health-related variables, measurements of harassment and bullying, and measurements of job satisfaction, leadership, and climate. In this study, only demographic questions and measurements of bullying and harassment are included. All surveys contained the question "Have you been subjected to bullying at the workplace during the last six months", with the following response categories: "No", "Yes, once or twice", "Yes, now and then", "Yes, about once a week", and "Yes, many times a week". In some surveys the options "Yes, monthly" and "Yes, several times a day", were also included. In this study the option "Yes, monthly" has been recoded to "Now and then", while all options from "Yes, about once a week", "Yes, many

TABLE 2
Main Demographical Characteristics of the Respondents in Each Subsample

		Age			
	Sex Ratio				Public
	Men:Women	Mean		Years of	Employment
Organization/Survey	(%)	(years)	SD	Service[a]	(%)
1. Teachers Union	39:61	41.6	9.0	10.0	99.3
2. Trade and Commerce	23:77	38.0	13.8	8.3	3.7
3. Clerical and Officials	22:78	41.8	12.5	9.0	92.3
4. Graphical Workers Union	85:15	41.4	12.4	14.1	6.5
5. Union of Hotel and Restaurant Workers	28:78	32.5	11.4	5.8	3.7
6. Employers Federation (NHO)	79:21	42.3	10.8	12.3	2.9
7. Electricians Union	97:3	33.4	10.8	9.2	0.4
8. University	52:48	–	–	11.7	98
9. Industrial Workers	98:2	43.3	11.5	15.4	100
10. Psychologists Union	60:40	39.5	11.2	–	–
11. Nursing Homes 1	6:94	43.0	–	–	100
12. Nursing Homes 2	3:97	42.0	–	–	100
13. Home-based Nursing	4:96	44.0	12.1	–	100
14. Health and Welfare Managers	55:45	46.0	–	–	100

[a]This refers only to the respondents' current employment, not to union membership seniority or to overall seniority in profession or working life.

times a week", and "Yes, several times a day" have been recoded and renamed to "Yes, weekly". All respondents were introduced to the following definition of bullying and harassment:

> Bullying (harassment, badgering, niggling, freezing out, offending someone) is a problem in some workplaces and for some workers. To label something bullying it has to occur repeatedly over a period of time, and the person confronted has to have difficulties defending himself/herself. It is not bullying if two parties of approximately equal "strength" are in conflict or the incident is an isolated event.

The definition, the question measuring bullying, the options, and the specified time frame of the period prevalence rate (previous six months) were adopted from research on bullying among children (Olweus, 1978, 1990, 1993, 1994; Olweus & Smith, 1995). The actual term used for bullying is the word "mobbing", the origin and use of which is discussed by Olweus (1990).

In addition, in most studies the respondents were also asked to indicate the duration of the bullying episode, the number of persons harassing them, the gender of their perpetrator(s), and whether the perpetrator(s) were immediate supervisor(s), manager(s), colleague(s) from their own work group or profession, colleague(s) from other work groups or professions, customer(s), student(s), or client(s).

RESULTS

Reported Prevalence and Duration of Bullying

Of the total sample of 7787 respondents, 7118 (91.4%) stated that they had not been bullied during the last six months. A total of 669 respondents (8.6%) reported being bullied during this period (Table 3). While 4.0% reported being bullied once of twice, 3.3% said that they were bullied now

TABLE 3
Overall Prevalence of Bullying During the Previous
Six Months

	Number of Respondents	Frequency (%)
No	7718	91.4
Yes, once or twice	309	4.0
Yes, now and then	263	3.4
Yes, weekly	96	1.2

and then. Another 1.2%, representing 96 respondents, reported being bullied on a weekly basis.

A total of 268 victims also indicated the duration of this current episode of bullying. Measurements of the duration of bullying were not included in samples 10, 11, and 14 (see Table 1). In addition, many victims responded inaccurately to this question by referring loosely to months or years. Among those 268 victims indicating an accurate duration, 41.8% responded that they had been bullied for a period of six months or less. Another 17.2% had already been victimized for between six and twelve months, while 23.9% had been bullied for more than two years. Mean duration was 18 months (SD 19.6). Table 4 shows the duration within the three different groups of victims. The results clearly show that the victims who are frequently bullied also report a longer duration of their problem, while the ones bullied seldomly report a shorter duration ($\chi^2 = 39.75$, $df = 6$, $P < 0.001$). Among those who were bullied weekly, 43.1% reported being bullied for more than two years, while another 25.5% had been bullied for more than one year.

Reported Bullies

Questions relating to who the bullies and perpetrators were conceived to be were not included in all studies (not in samples 14 and 11). A total of 469 victims identified their bullies or perpetrators. Thirty-eight percent claimed that they were bullied by colleagues within their own work group or their own profession. Another 23% reported colleagues from another work group or another profession to be the bully(ies). Altogether 54% of the victims reported one or more co-workers on their own organizational level as the perpetrator(s). Another 25% conceived the manager of the workplace to be a bully, while 28% reported being bullied by their immediate supervisor. About 25% also reported other leaders in the organization to be their bully. Altogether, 54% reported one or more superiors among the harassers. A total of 20% of the victims were bullied by both

TABLE 4
Duration of Bullying within Different Frequency Groups of Victims ($N = 268$)

	Less Than 7 Months (%)	From 7 to 12 Months (%)	From 13 to 24 Months (%)	More Than 24 Months (%)
Yes, once or twice	60.2	18.3	8.6	12.9
Yes, now and then	29.6	20.4	22.2	27.8
Yes, weekly	17.6	13.7	25.5	43.1

colleagues and supervisors/managers, while 68% were bullied either by colleagues or by superiors.

Altogether, 15% of the victims reported customers, clients, or students to be bullies, either as one of more bullies or the sole bully. Most of these victims were teachers in primary and secondary schools. Eighty percent of the victimized school teachers reported that their pupils were a significant part of their problem. In the total sample, equal numbers (15%) were bullied by a subordinate.

The victims were also asked to indicate the gender and the number of the perpetrator(s). A total of 392 victims responded to these questions. Forty-nine percent reported that they were bullied by one or more men, 30% that the perpetrator(s) were female, while 21% reported being bullied by both men and women. Less than half of the victims (42%) were bullied by only one person; 23% by only one man and 19% by only one woman. Table 5 shows the gender and the number of the bullies as reported by respectively male and female victims. Among male victims as many as 70% were bullied by men only, while 10% are bullied by women only. Most of the latter victims were bullied by only one woman. Female victims are to a larger degree bullied by both men and women. While 48% reported being bullied only by women, 31% reported men only as their bullies.

Risk Groups and Risk Organizations

A t-test yielded no significant difference in reported victimization between men and women ($t = 1.20$, $df = 7718$, $P > 0.05$). However, older employees reported significantly more bullying than younger ones ($\chi^2 = 17.03$, $df = 9$, $P < 0.05$). The prevalence rate among respondents younger than 45 years was 8.2%, whereas the prevalence rate among older respondents varied between 9.3% (61–65 years) and 10.3% (51–60 years). In some subsamples, the age difference was even more pronounced. However, in the University

TABLE 5
Perceived Bullies by Male and Female Victims (in percent)

	Male Victims (N = 176)					Female Victims (N = 204)				
	0 Men	1 Man	2 Men	3 Men	4–11 Men	0 Men	1 Man	2 Men	3 Men	4–11 Men
0 Women	–	30	12	12	16	–	18	7	3	3
1 Woman	7	9	3	–	0.5	30	7	2	0.5	0.5
2 Women	2	3	0	0.5	1	11	3	1	0.5	1
3 Women	0.5	0.5	0.5	1	0.5	3	0.5	0	2	1
4–10 Women	0.5	0.5	0	0	1	4	1	0	1	0

sample employees above 50 were significantly less bullied than younger employees.

In public companies significantly fewer respondents reported bullying than did those employed in private enterprises ($F = 10.95$, $df = 1$, $P < 0.001$). The prevalence rate in the public sector was 8.2%, while the prevalence rate was 10.7% among respondents in private organizations.

Table 6 shows the prevalence rates of reported bullying within each sub-sample. Significant differences in prevalence rates between the different samples and organizations were found. The highest prevalence rate was found among the industrial workers where 17.4% reported being bullied during the last six months. Bullying was also frequent among the graphical workers and the hotel and restaurant workers. The lowest rate of bullying was found among the psychologists and the university employees. The highest rate of the most frequent bullying (weekly or more often) was nevertheless found within trade and commerce (3.5%) and among clerical and officials (3.9%). A logistic regression analysis showed that these differences in prevalence rates were significant when controlled for response rate.

Although there were no significant differences between men and women when reporting bullying, the results clearly showed that the prevalence rates of bullying were highest in male-dominated organizations ($\chi^2 = 25.66$, $df = 4$, $P < 0.001$). While organizations dominated by men had a prevalence rate of 11.5%, female-dominated organizations had a prevalence rate

TABLE 6
Prevalence of Reported Bullying within Different Work Environments During Previous Six Months

Organization	Never (%)	Once or Twice (%)	Now and Then (%)	Weekly (%)
Teachers Union	91.7	4.0	2.0	2.4
Trade and Commerce	88.6	3.7	4.3	3.5
Clerical and Officials	87.2	5.1	3.9	3.9
Graphical Workers Union	84.8	4.4	8.9	1.9
Union of Hotel/Restaurant	85.9	7.1	4.1	2.9
Employers Federation (NFO)	90.2	6.9	2.3	0.6
Electricians Union	92.1	4.0	3.1	0.8
University	93.8	2.7	2.8	0.7
Industrial Workers	82.6	9.6	6.5	1.3
Psychologists Union	94.2	3.0	2.3	0.6
Health-care Workers[a]	92.4	4.3	2.2	1.1
Health/Welfare Managers	87.7	0.0	12.0	0.3

[a]This group consists of the three samples of nurses, nursing assistants, and other health-care workers working with the elderly within six different nursing homes and the home-based health and social services of a major Norwegian city (samples 11, 12, and 13).

of 7.5%. The frequency of bullying was also highest in workplaces with many employees ($\chi^2 = 19.82$, $df = 5$, $P < 0.01$). In workplaces with less than 10 employees, the frequency of bullying was 5.1%, while the frequency of bullying at workplaces with more than 50 employees was about 11%. However, only samples 1–7 and sample 12 provided information on this variable.

DISCUSSION

The presented findings indicate that bullying and harassment is a widespread problem in Norwegian working life. On average, 8.6% of the population consider themselves to be victims of bullying and harassment at work during the previous six months. For many of the victims, this has been a long-lasting problem. Mean duration of these episodes is 18 months. Hence, the bullying occurrences as reported by these victims are not isolated episodes or short conflict intermezzos, but rather ongoing situations where the victims repeatedly experience aggression from others at work. Thus, the result on duration may be interpreted as some validation of both the definition and the measurement of bullying used in the present study.

The measurement of bullying used in this study was adopted from research among Scandinavian schoolchildren (Olweus, 1978, 1990, 1993, 1994). Olweus (1990) defines a cutting point between those who report bullying "once or twice" and those who are bullied "now and then". To be considered bullied by Olweus, the student must respond that it happens "now and then" or more frequently (weekly or daily). Since the measurements, definitions, and prevalence period of the present studies were adopted from research on bullying among children, our results among adults may be directly compared to the results among children. Among children in primary schools, 11.5% of the pupils report being bullied now and then or more often. In junior high school (age 13 to 16) the frequency is 5.4% (Olweus, 1990). Using Olweus' criterion for selecting the victims, our results suggest a prevalence rate of 4.5% among adults, ranging from 2.9% among the psychologists to 12.3% among the health-care managers. In the sample of the industrial workers, where the response rate was very high (87%), as many as 7.8% reported bullying now and then or more often. Hence, the results indicate that bullying and harassment among adults may be as frequent as bullying among older children. In Scandinavia, results showing that at least 5% of the children are bullied are accepted as portraying an unacceptable level of bullying (O'Moore & Hillery, 1989).

The conclusion that some 4.5% of workers are victims of bullying does not differ much from results obtained in Sweden. On the basis of a large cross-sectional sample it is estimated that some 3.5% of the Swedish working population are victims of work harassment (*cf.* Leymann, 1992).

A study among Finnish governmental employees showed that some 10% had been bullied at least once a week for at least half a year (Vartia, 1991). Using weekly exposure as criterion for estimating exposure to bullying gives a prevalence rate as low as 1.2% in the present study. However, different definitions and measurements makes such comparisons difficult. The two mentioned studies defined bullying as the exposure to one or more out of 45 predefined behaviours on a weekly basis during a period of at least half a year (Leymann, 1990).

In the present study, older workers were at a higher risk of victimization than younger ones. While some 8.2% of participants younger than 50 reported some exposure to bullying, 10.3% of the participants between 51 and 60 years reported such victimization. This finding may however be interpreted in different ways. The most obvious explanation would be that older workers are in fact subjected to more aggressive acts than their younger colleagues. However, a study among male workers showed that older men reported significantly less exposure to potentially harassing behaviour than did younger workers (Einarsen & Raknes, 1995). In a study of a cross-sectional American adult sample, Felson (1992) found that younger individuals were more likely to be both aggressors and targets of aggression. Yet, Painter (1991) claims that any attempt to estimate incidence of violence at work must take the subjective evaluation and the physical and social vulnerability into account, as well as the social context of a particular incident. Thus, an alternative explanation may be that older workers are more vulnerable and/or have a lowered tolerance for such interactions. As employees grow older they may expect to be treated with more dignity and respect, hence lowering their threshold for what they regard as unacceptable behaviours from superiors and co-workers. Behaviours labelled by older workers as harassment may be interpreted by younger ones as innocent horseplay, a hazing ritual, or aggressive behaviour expected to be tolerated or managed. Older workers may also experience bullying more easily than younger ones due to difficulties in finding new employment. Aggressive treatment by colleagues or superiors may be perceived more severely if the victim is unable to escape the situation (Niedl, 1995).

More men than women were reported as bullies. Men were also more often than women reported to bully in groups. These results are similar to findings among schoolchildren. Olweus (1994) found that boys were more often bullies than girls, probably as a consequence of boys being more aggressive than girls. However, Björkqvist, Österman, and Lagerspetz (1994) claimed that there are no such gender differences in aggressiveness among adults. Instead, they proposed the "effect/danger ratio" as a cost/benefit model that can explain most variations in aggression. This ratio is an expression of the individual's estimation of the likely dangers and consequences of an aggressive act. Since men more often than women are in superior positions, and since leaders may experience less risk associated with aggressive enacting, this may explain the gender differences found in the present study. However, the fact that male-dominated organizations have more bullying than female-dominated organizations does challenge this explanation. More research is needed on this topic.

The results also indicate that men are harassed by men and women by women. These results are most probably due to the fact that Norwegian work life is gender segregated. This conclusion was also made by Leymann and Tallgren (1989) who found the same tendency in a Swedish steel company.

Moreover, large organizations or workplaces were found to have higher frequencies of bullying than smaller ones. In the field of sexual harassment it is also claimed that harassment is especially prevalent in large and hierarchical organizations (Einarsen, Raknes, & Matthiesen, 1993). According to the effect/danger ratio of Björkqvist and associates, the threshold of aggressive behaviour may be lowered in such organizations. The possibility of experiencing danger of social condemnation because of aggressive behaviour may be diminished both as a consequence of the size, the many layers of superiors, and the unequal distribution of power in these organizations. In small and transparent organizations both the perpetrator's risk of getting "caught" and the potential social consequences may be larger.

The results showing that victims of long-lasting bullying were bullied with the highest intensity may indicate that bullying takes the form of an escalating process. In the beginning the victims seem to be attacked only now and then. As the conflict escalates, the frequency of attacks increases and after some time the victims may be attacked on a weekly or even daily basis. Among victims reporting weekly exposure to bullying, 43% reported a duration of two years or more. Among those indicating that they were only bullied once or twice during the last six months, only 13% had been bullied for two years or more. As many as 60% of these victims had been bullied for half a year or less. In a study among Norwegian nurses and teachers, Matthiesen and colleagues (1989) concluded that victimization may be seen as a continuum from being not at all bullied to being heavily bullied. The present results indicate that this continuum may be strongly related to the duration of the bullying episode. These findings may also support theoretical notions describing bullying as the outcome of ill-managed and escalated conflicts (Einarsen, Raknes, Matthiesen, & Hellesøy, 1994; Leymann, 1990, 1992).

The victims in this study reported colleagues to be perpetrators as often as superiors. On the other hand, because leaders are few by numbers in most organizations, relatively more superiors are perceived as bullies compared to colleagues. Such a conclusion may easily be explained by the effect/danger ratio, and also coincides with findings from a Finnish university where individuals in superior positions were experienced as tormentors more often than individuals in subordinate positions (Björkqvist, Österman, & Hjelt-Bäck, 1994). A study among the male workforce of a marine maintenance workshop nevertheless suggested that different harassing behaviours were used by supervisors than by colleagues (Einarsen & Raknes, 1995). The terms "health-endangering leadership" (Kile, 1990), "petty tyrant" (Ashforth, 1994), "highly aggressive boss", and "militant managers" (Elbing & Elbing, 1994) have been used when describing how managers and supervisors may bully, harass, and torment their subordinates. The issue of collegial bullying versus leadership bullying must certainly be more deeply looked into in future research (see also Skogstad & Einarsen, submitted), as must differences between situations where there is only one bully and situations where a whole group is engaged in harassment. These situations may differ both in terms of aetiology, behaviours involved, and potential negative outcomes.

Some methodological concerns about the present study must be mentioned. First, the respondents in this study may not represent all sectors of Norwegian working life. Many types of organization and profession are not represented in this study, especially private enterprises. The unions and organizations chosen for these studies are nevertheless typical of large parts of Norwegian working life. None of the organizations or unions participated on the basis of any particular problem of harassment and bullying. However, since private enterprises may have higher prevalence than public organizations according to our results, more research should be conducted within such organizations.

In the present study, exposure to bullying and harassment at work was measured by presenting the respondents with a precise definition of the concept and then asking the participants whether or not they perceived themselves as victims of such bullying. This procedure has the advantage of giving the respondents a clear understanding of what they are to respond to, yielding rather specific response alternatives and specific time frames (Olweus, 1987, 1990). In addition, by measuring the global subjective perception and the individual construct of being victimized this method takes individual vulnerability into account. According to most definitions of bullying (see Björkqvist, Österman, & Hjelt-Bäck, 1994; Niedl, 1995; O'Moore & Hillery, 1989; Olweus, 1990) it is important to differentiate both between negative behaviours that are tolerated and behaviours that are not tolerated, and between situations that can be handled and situations where the victims have difficulties defending themselves. The global perception of being bullied and victimized may relate more directly to negative outcomes and consequences than do the actual behaviours involved (Painter, 1991; Terpstra & Baker, 1987). However, a disadvantage of the measurement used is the lack of information regarding the kinds of acts and behaviours involved.

Moreover, this method of measuring bullying may be criticized for being too subjective (see Frese & Zapf, 1988) and hence highly related to third variables such as negative affectivity (Burke, Brief, & George, 1993). However, research among children suggests that this is not the case. In a study among children aged 10 to 13, Olweus (1987) investigated whether this method gave an exaggerated picture of the frequency of bullying problems by relating the self-reports of some 2000 students with the reports of 90 form masters and mistresses assessing which of these students were bullied in their classes. The agreement between teacher ratings and the self-reports were striking. Only a difference in the order of 1–2% was found, indicating that perceptions of observers of bullying correspond closely to the respective victims' self-report. A study among adults focusing on the relationships between bullying and perceived work environment quality showed that both victims and observers of bullying reported a low quality work environment. Hence, participants who were not bullied themselves but who had observed others being bullied, validated the perceptions of the victims (Einarsen, Raknes, & Matthiesen, 1994).

Yet, harassment may be difficult to quantify using people's perceptions, in part because people tend to deny or minimize abuse as a way to survive in an abusive environment (Randall, 1992). Hence, such a highly subjective measure of exposure to bullying may in fact produce an underestimation of the problem. To admit to being a victim of work harassment is to admit to weakness and inadequate coping, which may be difficult and self-esteem threatening for most people (O'Moore & Hillery, 1989). In a study among female university faculties, 88% of the women had encountered behaviours legally defined as sexual harassment, although only 5.6% confirmed that they felt sexually harassed (Brooks & Perot, 1991).

Hence, in future research both measurements of exposure to potentially harassing behaviours and the subjective perception of victimization should be included (Fitzgerald & Shullman, 1993). Future studies on the prevalence of bullying should also include observer/victim reliability investigations and peer nomination techniques (see also Björkqvist, Österman, & Hjelt-Bäck, 1994; Olweus, 1978, 1987), which would provide additional objective data on the frequency of bullying at work.

ACKNOWLEDGEMENTS

This research was in part supported by a grant from the Norwegian Employers Association (NHO). We are also grateful to all participating organizations and labour unions for their financial and logistical support of these studies. Thanks to our colleagues at the Division of Work and Organizational Psychology for their co-operation and contributions in the surveys presented in this article. Special thanks are due to Professor Jan Forslin and to three reviewers for their comments on an earlier draft of the manuscript.

REFERENCES

Adams, A. (1992). *Bullying at work: How to confront and overcome it.* London: Virago Press.

Ashforth, B. (1994). Petty tyranny in organizations. *Human Relations, 47*, 755–778.

Björkqvist, K., Österman, K., & Hjelt-Bäck, M. (1994). Aggression among university employees. *Aggressive Behavior, 20*, 173–184.

Björkqvist, K., Österman, K., & Lagerspetz, K.M.J. (1994). Sex differences in covert aggression among adults. *Aggressive Behavior, 20*, 27–33.

Brodsky, C.M. (1976). *The harassed worker.* Toronto: Lexington Books, DC Heath & Company.

Brooks, L., & Perot, A.R. (1991). Reporting sexual harassment: Exploring a predictive model. *Psychology of Women Quarterly, 15*, 31–47.

Burke, M.J., Brief, A.P., & George, J.M. (1993). The role of negative affectivity in understanding relations between self-reports of stressors and strains: A comment on the applied psychology literature. *Journal of Applied Psychology, 78*, 402–412.

Einarsen, S., & Raknes, B.I. (1995, April). *Harassment at work and the victimization of men.* Paper presented as a poster at the Seventh European Congress on Work and Organizational Psychology, Györ, Hungary.

Einarsen, S., Raknes, B.I., & Matthiesen, S.B. (1993). *Seksuell trakassering [Sexual harassment].* Bergen, Norway: Sigma Forlag.

Einarsen, S., Raknes, B.I., & Matthiesen, S.B. (1994). Bullying and harassment at work and their relationships to work environment quality: An exploratory study. *The European Work and Organizational Psychologist, 4*, 381–401.

Einarsen, S., Raknes, B.I., Matthiesen, S.B., & Hellesøy, O.H. (1994). *Mobbing og personkonflikter. Helsefarlig samspill på arbeidsplassen [Bullying and personified conflicts: Health-endangering interaction at work].* Bergen, Norway: Sigma Forlag.

Elbing, C., & Elbing, A. (1994). *Militant managers.* New York: Irwin Professional Publishing.

Felson, R.B. (1992). "Kick 'em when they're down": Explanations of the relationships between stress and interpersonal aggression and violence. *Sociological Quarterly, 33*, 1–16.

Fitzgerald, L.F., & Shullman, S.L. (1993). Sexual harassment: A research analysis and agenda for the 1990s. *Journal of Vocational Behavior, 42*, 5–27.

Frese, M., & Zapf, D. (1988). Methodological issues in the study of work stress: Objective vs. subjective measurements of work stress and the question of longitudinal studies. In C.L. Cooper & R. Payne (Eds.), *Causes, coping, and consequences of stress at work* (pp. 371–411). Chichester: Wiley.

Heinemann, P. (1972). *Mobbing—grippvald [Mobbing—group violence].* Stockholm: Nature & Kultur.

Kaye, K. (1994). *Workplace wars and how to end them: Turning personal conflicts into productive teamwork.* New York: Amacom.

Kile, S.M. (1990). *Helsefarlige ledere og medarbeidere [Health injuring leaders and co-workers].* Oslo, Norway: Hjemmets Bokforlag.

Leymann, H. (1990). Mobbing and psychological terror at workplaces. *Violence and Victims, 5*, 119–126.

Leymann, H. (1991). *Medling och psykosocial rehabilitering [Arbitration and psychosocial rehabilitation].* Stockholm: Allmänna Förlaget.

Leymann, H. (1992). *Från mobbning til utslagning i arbetslivet [From bullying to exclusion from working life].* Stockholm: Publica.

Leymann, H., & Gustavsson, B. (1984). *Psykiskt våld i arbetslivet.* Stockholm: Arbetarskyddsstyrelsen.

Leymann, H., & Tallgren, U. (1989). Undersökning av frekvensen av vuxenmobbning innom SSAB med en nytt frågeformular [An investigation of the frequency of bullying in SSAB with a new questionnaire]. *Arbete, Människa, Miljö, 1*, 3–12.

Matthiesen, S.B. (1990, July). *Bullying at the worksite*. Paper presented at the Fourth European Conference on Health Psychology, Oxford.

Matthiesen, S.B., Raknes, B.I., & Rökkum, O. (1989). Mobbing på arbeidsplassen [Bullying at work]. *Tidsskrift for Norsk Psykologforening, 26*, 761–774.

Niedl, K. (1995). *Mobbing/bullying am Arbeitsplatz [Mobbing/bullying at work]*. München: Rainer Hampp Verlag.

O'Moore, A.M., & Hillery, B. (1989). Bullying in Dublin schools. *Irish Journal of Psychology, 10*, 426–441.

Olweus, D. (1978). *Aggression in the schools: Bullies and whipping boys*. Washington, DC: Hemisphere, Wiley.

Olweus, D. (1987). Bully/victims problems among schoolchildren in Scandinavia. In J.P. Myklebust & R. Ommundsen (Eds.), *Psykologprofesjonen mot år 2000* (pp. 395–413). Oslo: Universitetsforlaget.

Olweus, D. (1989). Prevalence and incidence in the study of antisocial behavior: Definitions and measurements. In M.W. Klein (Ed.), *Cross-national research in self reported crime and delinquency* (pp. 187–201). Dorndrect: Kluwer.

Olweus, D. (1990). Bully/victim problems among schoolchildren: Basic facts and effects of a school based intervention program. In K. Rubin & D. Pepler (Eds.), *The development and treatment of children's aggression*. Hillsdale, NJ: Lawrence Erlbaum Associates Inc.

Olweus, D. (1993). *Bullying at school: What we know and what we can do*. Oxford: Blackwell Publishers.

Olweus, D. (1994). Annotation: Bullying at school—Basic facts and effects of a school based intervention program. *Journal of Child Psychology and Psychiatry, 35*, 1171–1190.

Olweus, D., & Smith, P.K. (1995). *Manual of the Olweus bully/victim questionnaire*. Oxford: Blackwell Publishers.

Painter, K. (1991). Violence and vulnerability in the workplace: Psychosocial and legal implications. In M.J. Davidson & J. Earnshaw (Eds.), *Vulnerable workers: Psychosocial and legal issues* (pp. 160–178). New York: John Wiley & Sons.

Randall, T. (1992). Abuse at work drains people, money, and medical workplace not immune. *Journal of the American Medical Association, 267*, 1439–1440.

Roland, E. (1989). Bullying: The Scandinavian research tradition. In D.P. Tattum & D.A. Lane (Eds.), *Bullying in schools*. London: Trenthan Books.

Roland, E., & Munthe, E. (1989). *Bullying: An international perspective*. London: Davis Fulton Publishers.

Skogstad, A., & Einarsen, S. (submitted). *Relationships between leadership behavior, and subordinates' job satisfaction and subjective health*.

Terpstra, D.E., & Baker, D.D. (1987). Psychological and demographic correlates of perception of sexual harassment. *Genetic, Social and General Psychological Monographs, 112*, 459–478.

Vartia, M. (1991). Bullying at workplaces. In S. Lehtinene, J. Rantanen, P. Juuti, A. Koskela, K. Lindström, P. Rehnström, & J. Saari (Eds.), *Towards the 21st century: Work in the 1990s: Proceedings from the International Symposium on Future Trends in the Changing Working Life*. Helsinki: Institute of Occupational Health.

EUROPEAN JOURNAL OF WORK AND ORGANIZATIONAL PSYCHOLOGY, 1996, 5 (2), 203–214

The Sources of Bullying—Psychological Work Environment and Organizational Climate

Maarit Vartia

Department of Psychology, Institute of Occupational Health, Vantaa, Finland

The aim of this study was to identify the work-related risks of bullying in the psychological work environment and the organizational climate. Also the role of some individual and personality characteristics in becoming a victim of bullying were investigated. Altogether 949 municipal employees answered a mailed questionnaire; 10.1% of them felt themselves bullied. Especially some features in the functioning of the work unit, e.g. poor information flow, an authoritative way of settling differences of opinion, lack of mutual conversations about the tasks and goals of the work unit, and insufficient possibilities to influence matters concerning oneself can all promote bullying. Both the victims and the observers of bullying perceived deficiencies in these aspects at their workplace. Gender and age did not explain bullying. The victims of bullying felt that envy, a weak superior, competition for tasks or advancement, and competition for the supervisor's favour and approval were the most common reasons for bullying.

Social interaction at work, the relationships between co-workers as well as between supervisors and other employees, is of great importance to everybody in many ways. Good interpersonal relationships are connected with job satisfaction. Social support from the superior or from one's co-workers helps to build up individual resources. Interpersonal conflicts between people can, on the other hand, become a significant source of work stress (e.g. Cooper & Marshall, 1976; House, 1981). Bullying or mobbing is one form of extreme negative social interaction at work.

The meaning of the work environment and of leadership in the bullying process, and the importance of identifying the work-related risk factors connected with bullying, have been emphasized especially by Scandinavian researchers (Björkqvist, Österman, & Hjelt-Bäck, 1994; Einarsen, Raknes, & Matthiesen, 1994; Leymann, 1992a). Very little research has, however, been done so far in this field. In the study by Einarsen et al. (1994) particu-

Requests for reprints should be addressed to M. Vartia, Institute of Occupational Health, Laajaniityntie 1, SF-01620 Vantaa, Finland. Email: mvar@occuphealth.fi

larly role conflict, but also low satisfaction with leadership, work control, and social climate, correlated with bullying. Both the victims themselves and the witnesses or "observers" of bullying expressed dissatisfaction with their work environment. Bullying was related to different aspects of the work environment in different kinds of organizations.

Basing on a large number of individual cases, Leymann (1992a) establishes that the bullying process starts from a conflict. He has introduced the following development of the process: severe stress factors related to the work organization (and to leadership)→frustration→letting out one's feelings→psychological terror. Thylefors (1987) describes bullying as a scapegoating process. She sees bullying as a complicated interactive process in which the organization, the group, and the victim each have a specific role.

Harassment or mobbing at work has also been related to the type of work. People working in administration and services were mobbed more often than those in research and teaching or in production (Björkqvist et al., 1994; Leymann, 1992b).

In everyday life, on the other hand, people tend to find sources of interpersonal conflicts in personality characteristics rather than in environmental factors. In connection with bullying, the individual characteristics of both the harassed and the harasser have been discussed by Adams (1992) and by Brodsky (1976). Brodsky (1976) describes the bullied as, for example, conscientious, literal-minded, and somewhat unsophisticated, often overachievers who have an unrealistic view of themselves. He describes some harassed persons as paranoid, some as rigid, and some as compulsive individuals. Adams (1992) suggested sadism, narcissism, and envy to be related to bullying. The descriptions of Brodsky and Adams are grounded on the opinions and descriptions of the victims, and therefore ought to be interpreted very cautiously. No systematic studies on the personality characteristics of the bullies have been done so far.

The results of the causes of bullying, as experienced by the victims, vary. Among university employees, the victims perceived the reasons of bullying to emerge from the competition for jobs and status, personality factors of both the tormentor and the victim, and envy (Björkqvist et al., 1994). The most common reasons quoted by Zapf, Knorz, and Kulla (1995) were: "They want to push me out of the company" and "A certain person influenced others". Next came organizational reasons: "Organizational climate", "Unresolved conflict", and "High stress".

The purpose of this study was to identify the work-related risks of bullying in the psychological work environment and the features of the organizational climate. The connections between bullying and some individual and personality factors were also analysed. As very few studies have been focused on these questions, this study was mainly explorative in nature.

MATERIAL AND METHOD

Sample

A questionnaire was mailed to 1577 members of the Finnish Federation of Municipal Officials. Every 35th member of the union was selected for the study. The questionnaire was sent to their home address. After an additional request, altogether 1037 persons (65.8%) returned the questionnaire. Eighty-eight of these were removed from the study group because of long-term unemployment or absence from work. The final study group comprised 949 respondents, of whom 85% were women and 15% were men. This reflects well with the membership of the union (in 1993, 85.1% women, 14.9% men). The mean age of the respondents was 40 years (SD 10.15), and they worked in a large variety of occupations. The largest group consisted of office workers (48%); 12% worked in food services and basic servicing tasks. Of all the respondents, 42% had worked for over 10 years in their present work unit, 20% from five to ten years, 17% from three to five years, and 21% for less than two years.

Measures

The questionnaire comprised altogether 149 questions. The following definition of bullying was given at the beginning of the questionnaire:

> Bullying is long-lasting, recurrent, and serious negative actions, and behaviour that is annoying and oppressing. It is not bullying if you are scolded once or somebody shrugs his/her shoulders at you once. Negative behaviour develops into bullying when it becomes continuous and repeated. Often the victim of bullying feels unable to defend him/herself.

After this definition the respondents were asked if they felt themselves to be subjected to this kind of bullying. The forms of bullying (e.g. people refuse to talk with you, people spread false and groundless information about you, people shout at you, you are threatened by physical violence) were measured using a revised version of the Leymann Inventory of Psychological Terrorization (LIPT; Leyman, 1989). In order to be considered as a victim of bullying, the respondent had to answer "yes" to the general bullying question and to have been subjected often to at least one single form of bullying. The respondents were also asked if there was someone else at their workplace who was being bullied.

The characteristics of work (monotony, autonomy at work, haste at work, possibilities to influence matters concerning oneself) were measured by single questions from the Occupational Stress Questionnaire (OSQ) developed at the Finnish Institute of Occupational Health. The response format in each item was a five-point Likert scale (Elo, Leppänen,

Lindström, & Ropponen, 1992). The OSQ is widely used in Finland. Studies of the measurement properties of the questionnaire, including reliability and validity, have been reviewed by Elo et al. (1992).

Mutual discussions about the tasks and goals at work were enquired about by one question: "How often do you discuss your tasks and the goals of your work, and the attainment of the goals together at your workplace?" One item measured the type of problem solving in the work unit: "How are differences of opinion usually settled at your workplace?" The alternatives to this were (1) by talking over the matter and by negotiating, (2) by taking advantage of one's position or authority or by order, and (3) we do not try to settle them at all. The alternatives were dichotomized for the further analyses.

The general atmosphere of the work unit was measured by a question with five fixed alternatives. For further analyses this variable was also transformed into five dichotomized variables. The anticipated changes at work were also measured by the item: "Are you aware of big changes at your workplace in the near future (e.g. organizational changes, new working methods, notice of termination)?"

The features of organizational climate were measured by a list of statements (e.g. "Everybody is listened to at my workplace", "Workmates compete with each other", "There is envy at my workplace", "Independence is appreciated and encouraged at my workplace", "Personal differences are accepted at my workplace"). The response format was a three-point scale from "fully agree" to "do not agree". A factor analysis (Maximum Likelihood) and varimax rotation was conducted, revealing two factors (Table 1). Two scales were formed according to the factor analysis and labelled "Communication climate" and "Social climate". Both scales had good internal consistency (Cronbach's alpha 0.83 and 0.81).

Self-esteem was measured by Rosenberg's self-esteem scale with 10 items (Robinson, Shaver, & Wrightsman, 1991), and neuroticism and extro-

TABLE 1
Factor Structure of the Organizational Climate

	Factor Loadings
Factor 1: Communication Climate	
Everybody is listened to at my workplace	0.74
Problems at work and differences of opinion are discussed openly	0.72
Everybody has the courage to express his/her opinion	0.67
Independence is appreciated and encouraged	0.62
Personal differences are accepted	0.52
Factor 2: Social Climate	
There is envy at my workplace	0.83
Workmates compete with each other	0.66
There are cliques and underestimation of others at my workplace	0.66

version–introversion by the MPI (Minnesota Personality Inventory) with 12 items.

The results were analysed by comparing the following groups: (1) the bullied respondents, (2) those who were not bullied themselves but who reported that there was someone else bullied at their workplace, i.e. the witnesses, and (3) those who reported that nobody was bullied at their workplace, i.e. the "no-bullying" group. Einarsen et al. (1994) called the respondents of group 2 "observers", and the same term is used in this article.

RESULTS

Occurrence of Bullying

Altogether 10.1% of the respondents felt themselves bullied, 8.7% were observers, and 81.1% worked at no-bullying workplaces. Among the victims there were no differences between men and women.

Perceived Reasons of Bullying

Envy, a weak superior, competition for tasks or advancement, and competition for the superior's favour and approval were most often perceived as reasons for bullying. About one out of five victims felt that being different from the others was the reason why they had become victims of bullying. Only a few victims perceived unsatisfactory and monotonous work as a reason for bullying (Table 2).

The General Atmosphere at Work

At the bullying workplaces, the general atmosphere was most often experienced as strained and competitive, with everybody pursuing their own interests. At the no-bullying workplaces, the atmosphere was most often

TABLE 2
Reasons for Bullying as Experienced by the
Bullied Individuals

Reason	Yes, much (N = 95)
Envy	63%
Weak superior	42%
Competition for tasks or advancement	38%
Competition for the superior's favour and approval	34%
Insecurity (e.g. risk of losing one's job)	23%
Age (oldest, youngest)	22%
Being different from others	21%
Unsatisfactory and monotonous work	7%

easy-going and pleasant. A prejudiced atmosphere that clings to old ways did not predict bullying (Table 3).

Type of Problem Solving

The way in which differences of opinion are settled at the workplace seemed to be an important functional variable behind bullying. At bullying workplaces, differences of opinion were most often settled by taking advantage of one's position or authority, or by order. At the no-bullying workplaces, differences of opinion were usually settled by talking over the matter and by negotiating. The differences between the three groups were statistically very significant (Table 4).

TABLE 3
General Atmosphere at the Workplace

	Bullied (N = 81) %	Observers (N = 70) %	No Bullying (N = 682) %	x^2
Strained and competitive, everybody pursues their own interest	42	21	10	67.94*
Encouraging and supportive	4	13	19	13.03*
Prejudiced, clings to old ways	27	34	26	2.44[ns]
Easy-going and comfortable	7	21	42	46.04*
Quarrelsome, sullen; people do not get along with one another	19	10	3	42.51*
Total	100	100	100	

*$P < 0.001$; [ns] = not significant.

TABLE 4
How Differences of Opinion are Settled at Work

	Bullied (N = 88) %	Observers (N = 76) %	No Bullying (N = 736) %	x^2
By talking over the matter and by negotiating	23	37	69	91.07**
By taking advantage of one's position or authority, or by order	55	50	21	70.10**
No attempt to solve them	23	13	11	10.71*
Total	100	100	100	

*$P < 0.01$; **$P < 0.001$.

Psychological Work Environment

Regarding the features of the psychological work environment, especially the lack of possibilities to influence matters concerning oneself, poor flow of information at work, and lack of mutual conversations about tasks and goals, proved to associate strongly with bullying. Statistically significant differences were found between the bullied and the no-bullying group, but also between the observers and the no-bullying group (Table 5). The goals of one's own work were more often unclear to the victims compared to the observers or the no-bullying group, but no difference was found between the observers and the no-bullying group.

The attitude towards innovations was associated with bullying. Both the victims and the observers of bullying experienced the attitude towards innovations at their workplace as more negative compared with employees from the no-bullying workplaces.

The features of the work (haste, autonomy, monotony) were perceived most negatively by the bullied persons. No differences were found between the observers and the no-bullying group.

The anticipation of forthcoming big changes at work seemed to promote bullying. The differences between the three study groups were statistically significant ($\chi^2 = 18.758$, $df = 2$, $P < 0.001$). Altogether 63% of the bullied, 68% of the observers, and 48% of the respondents from the no-bullying group reported that they were anticipating big changes concerning their work unit in the near future.

Organizational Climate

Both the communication climate and the social climate were found to be associated with bullying. There were significant differences in the climate factors between the three study groups (see Table 5). Multiple regression analysis was conducted revealing that psychological work environment factors, anticipation of forthcoming changes, general atmosphere, and organizational climate factors explained 24% of the variance in bullying (Table 6).

Individual and Personality Traits

Gender did not correlate with bullying, and the correlation between age and bullying was very slight (−0.08). Significant correlations were found between bullying and neuroticism and self-esteem. When the psychological work environment and climate factors were kept constant the significance of the personality factors disappeared (Table 6). No differences in extro-version–introversion were found between the respondents in the three groups.

TABLE 5

Comparison of the Psychological Work Environment, Organizational Climate, and Individual and Personality Characteristics of the Bullied, Observers, and the No-bullying Group

	Bullied		Observers		No-bullying		F-value (df = 2)	P	P Bullied/ Observers	P Bullied/ No-bullying	P Observers/ No-bullying
	M	SD	M	SD	M	SD					
Possibilities to influence matters concerning oneself	3.40	0.99	3.00	1.00	2.57	0.92	38.10	0.0001	0.005	0.0001	0.0001
Flow of information	3.65	1.13	3.23	1.06	2.77	1.03	34.17	0.0001	0.008	0.0001	0.0002
Mutual discussions about tasks and goals	3.47	1.12	3.06	1.09	2.76	1.07	20.44	0.0001	0.011	0.0001	0.015
Clarity of goals in one's own work	2.16	0.98	1.71	0.82	1.67	0.71	17.93	0.0001	0.0001	0.0001	0.628
Attitude towards innovations	2.24	0.61	2.04	0.55	1.91	0.62	18.95	0.0001	0.026	0.0001	0.010
Haste at work	3.84	0.82	3.49	0.98	3.41	0.88	10.02	0.0001	0.009	0.0001	0.430
Autonomy at work	2.21	0.93	1.94	0.65	1.96	0.74	5.00	0.007	0.016	0.002	0.855
Perceived monotony	2.36	0.82	2.05	0.87	2.14	0.82	3.61	0.027	0.013	0.018	0.314
Communication climate	16.86	2.42	15.00	2.75	13.05	3.29	67.25	0.0001	0.0001	0.0001	0.0001
Social climate	4.75	1.54	5.69	1.73	6.93	1.69	85.39	0.0001	0.0002	0.0001	0.0001

TABLE 6
Pearson Product-moment Correlations between Bullying and the Study Variables and
Partial Correlations after Multiple Regression Analysis

Predictor	Correlation Coefficients ($N = 913$)	Beta Coefficients
Differences of opinion are settled by taking advantage of one's position or authority, or by order	-0.27***	-0.078*
The atmosphere is trained and competitive	-0.29***	-0.182***
The atmosphere is quarrelsome, sullen	-0.23***	-0.187***
Changes at work are anticipated	-0.13***	-0.077*
Communication climate	-0.36***	-0.097*
Social climate	-0.39***	0.167***
Gender	0.00ns	-0.023ns
Age	-0.08*	-0.011ns
Neuroticism	-0.14***	-0.004ns
Self-esteem	0.14***	0.054ns

$R^2 = 0.24$; R^2adj. $= 0.23$; $F = 22.03$; $P < 0.0001$; ns = not significant; *$P < 0.05$; **$P < 0.01$; ***$P < 0.001$.

DISCUSSION

The study showed that the risk factors of bullying at work can be found in the psychological work environment and organizational climate. An authoritative way of settling differences of opinion at work, poor possibilities to influence matters concerning oneself, poor flow of information, and lack of mutual discussions about tasks and goals proved to be important characteristics of a work environment which promotes bullying. Also the attitude towards innovations was connected to bullying. The results concerning the communication climate demonstrate the importance of discussions, listening, and tolerance.

It is important to note that not only the victims, but also the observers of bullying experienced a deficiency in these areas. The victims of bullying may after long-lasting negative treatment tend to describe their work environment very negatively in every respect. On the other hand, bullying may have worsened their work tasks and work environment as a whole, so the reports of the observers are of great importance.

Many of the environmental characteristics describe the functional features of a work unit. Most of them are also factors related to the leadership style and supervisory practices. This means that the supervisor has the power to influence and develop these aspects in the work unit.

The present findings confirm and complement the results of the Norwegian study which showed that particularly role conflict, but also leadership, work control, and social climate, correlated with bullying (Einarsen et al., 1994). The social climate factors, however, were different in the two studies. This study confirms also the Norwegian results concerning the connection between goal clarity and bullying.

The features of work were perceived most negatively by the victims, compared with the observers and the no-bullying group. The victims did not, however, experience unsatisfactory and monotonous work as a real cause of bullying. These results can have several explanations. First, the results can mean that the features of work are not connected to bullying. Second, giving monotonous tasks, giving too much work, and preventing autonomy are often forms of bullying. The third explanation could be that after being treated negatively for a long time, the victims of bullying perceive and report negatively all aspects of their work and work environment.

There were more often anticipated changes at work at bullying workplaces compared with the no-bullying workplaces. The economic depression and changes at work during the past few years in Finland has led to a situation in which the number of personnel has decreased and the stress of the employees increased. The difficult situation at workplaces and the uncertainty due to anticipated changes can also promote bullying at work.

Significant differences were found in the general atmosphere between the workplaces with and without bullying. One explanation for this is that a strained and competitive or quarrelsome and sullen atmosphere creates bullying. The other explanation is that a strained or quarrelsome atmosphere is a consequence of bullying. The cross-sectional study design makes it very difficult to interpret these results. The same intepretation problem is encountered with the personality characteristics in the bullying process.

Neuroticism and self-esteem correlated with bullying; the victims of bullying seemed to be more neurotic and to have a lower self-esteem than the not-bullied employees. This connection disappeared, however, when the work environment and climate factors were kept constant. This implies that the original correlation was not real. Neuroticism and self-esteem were correlated with communication (0.21, −0.16) and social climate (−0.18, 0.15) factors.

If we see bullying as a process at the workplace, the work environment and personality factors may play different roles at different stages of this process. Problems in the work environment and in leadership style can burst out as a conflict between employees, and later, if the conflict is not resolved, expand to bullying. At the stage when the victim is "selected", personality factors can be of importance. Further investigation and different study methods and designs (longitudinal studies, intensive case studies) are, however, needed to get a better understanding of the role and meaning of personality factors in the bullying process.

The victims themselves experienced envy, a weak superior, and competition as the main reasons for bullying. Envy and competition were also perceived as the most common reasons for bullying in a study among university employees (Björkqvist et al., 1994). Envy was not mentioned as a separate cause of bullying in the German study of Zapf et al. (1995) but there may be envy behind some of the reasons reported, e.g. "They wanted to push me out of the company".

The differences found in the causes of bullying perceived by the victims in the Finnish and in the German studies could be due to the fixed alternatives that were presented. In the present study as well as in the studies of Björkqvist et al. (1994) and Zapf et al. (1995) a list of plausible reasons for harassment was presented to the subjects. The alternatives selected by the researchers were somewhat different in the Finnish studies from those in the German study. Also the type of organization plays a contributing role. At a university, competition is always present in many ways, and it is natural that it is also experienced as a reason for bullying and harassment (Björkqvist et al., 1994).

In everyday work life, being different from the others is often expressed as a reason for bullying. In the present study, however, only one out of five victims of bullying felt that being different from the others was a reason for having been victimized.

In the present study 24% of the variance in bullying could be explained. In future studies, especially the meaning of the organizational culture, the things that the organization values, and for which it rewards or punishes, should be investigated more thoroughly. Also stress factors outside work can relate to interpersonal conflicts and bullying (Appelberg, Romanov, Honkasalo, & Koskenvuo, 1991). These have so far been studied very little (Niedl, 1995).

Bullying at work is still a difficult topic of discussion at workplaces. The discussion drifts easily to personality factors and to accusations. In many cases the victims themselves also begin to think that they themselves are guilty, or that being subjected to bullying is their own fault. Knowledge about the work-related variables behind bullying can help the victims to handle the situation.

The conception that people have of the sources of bullying gives direction also to the actions planned to prevent and solve bullying problems at work. Investigation, but also training and communication are therefore important. When the supervisors and organizations are aware of the different environmental risks of bullying, much can be done to prevent bullying at work.

REFERENCES

Adams, A. (1992). *Bullying at work: How to confront and overcome it*. London: Virago Press.
Appelberg, K., Romanov, K., Honkasalo, M.-L., & Koskenvuo, M. (1991). Interpersonal conflicts at work and psychosocial characteristics of employees. *Social Science Medicine*, *32*, 1051–1056.

Björkqvist, K., Österman, K., & Hjelt-Bäck, M. (1994). Aggression among university employees. *Aggressive Behavior, 20*, 173–184.

Brodsky, C.M. (1976). *The harassed worker*. Toronto: Lexington Books, DC Heath & Company.

Cooper, C.L., & Marshall, J. (1976). Occupational sources of stress: A review of the literature relating to coronary heart disease and mental ill health. *Journal of Occupational Psychology, 49*, 11–28.

Einarsen, S., Raknes, B.I., & Matthiesen, S.B. (1994). Bullying and harassment at work and their relationship to work environment quality: An exploratory study. *The European Work and Organizational Psychologist, 4*(4), 381–401.

Elo, A.-L., Leppänen, A., Lindström, K., & Ropponen, T. (1992). *Occupational stress questionnaire: User's instructions*. Helsinki: Institute of Occupational Health.

House, J.S. (1981). *Work stress and social support*. Reading, MA: Addison-Wesley.

Leymann, H. (1989). *Presentation av LIPT-formuläret. Konstruktion, validering, utfall. [Presentation of the Leymann Inventory for Psychological Terrorization]*. Stockholm: Violen inom Praktikertjänst.

Leymann, H. (1992a). *Från mobbning till utslagning i arbetslivet [From bullying to exclusion from working life]*. Stockholm: Publica.

Leymann, H. (1992b). *Vuxenmobbning på svenska arbetsplatser [Adult bullying in Swedish workplaces]*. Solna: Arbetarskyddsstyrelsen.

Niedl, K. (1995). *Mobbing/Bullying am Arbeitsplatz [Mobbing/bullying at work]*. München: Rainer Hampp Verlag.

Robinson, J.P., Shaver, P.R., & Wrightsman, L.S. (Eds.). (1991). *Measures of personality and social psychological attitudes*. Measures of Psychological Attitude Series: Vol. 1. New York: Academic Press.

Thylefors, I. (1987). *Syndabockar. Om utstötning och mobbning i arbetslivet. [Scapegoats: On exclusions and bullying in working life]*. Stockholm: Natur och Kultur.

Zapf, D., Knorz, C., & Kulla, M. (1995, April). *Causes and consequences of various mobbing factors at work*. Paper presented at the Seventh European Congress of Work and Organizational Psychology, Györ, Hungary.

EUROPEAN JOURNAL OF WORK AND ORGANIZATIONAL PSYCHOLOGY, 1996, 5 (2), 215–237

On the Relationship between Mobbing Factors, and Job Content, Social Work Environment, and Health Outcomes

Dieter Zapf

University of Konstanz, Germany

Carmen Knorz

University of Giessen, Germany

Matthias Kulla

University of Bielefeld, Germany

This article analyses the relationship between mobbing, job characteristics, social environment variables, and psychological ill-health. The Leymann Inventory of Psychological Terrorization (LIPT) was factor analysed and led to seven factors in two samples of mobbing victims ($N = 50$ and $N = 99$): Mobbing by organizational measures, social isolation, attacking the victim's private life, attacking the victim's attitudes, physical violence, verbal aggression, and rumours. Mobbing was correlated with bad job content, a bad social environment, and psychological ill-health. The findings suggest that the more social support supervisors gave, the less the victims reported being shouted at, being constantly criticized, and receiving verbal threats. In contrast, the more social support the victims received from their colleagues the less they reported being socially isolated or being ridiculed with regard to their private life. Moreover, having private life attacked showed the strongest correlation with psychological ill-health. The data suggest that organizational factors are potential causes of mobbing at work.

The concept of mobbing was introduced in Germany by Heinz Leymann (1993a, 1993b, 1995, this issue) at the beginning of the 1990s, about 10 years after its introduction in Scandinavia. It stands for the severe form of harassing people in organizations. Theoretically, mobbing is an extreme form of social stressors at work. It is amazing both from the scientist's and the practitioner's point of view that there was so little prior research in this area.

Requests for reprints should be addressed to D. Zapf, Universität Konstanz, Social-wissenschaftliche Fakultät, Arbeits- & Organisationspsychologie, Post-box 5560, D42, D-78434 Konstanz, Germany. Email: dieter.zapf@uni-konstanz.de

Scientifically, psychological stress research outside organizations was done primarily in a social context with stressors typically of a social nature (e.g. Dohrenwend & Dohrenwend, 1974; Lazarus & Folkman, 1984). In contrast, organizational stress research had its main focus on environmental, organizational, and task-related stressors (see, for example, Kahn & Byosiere, 1992).

There is, of course, some empirical evidence on the importance of social stressors in comparison to other stressors in organizations. Schwartz and Stone (1993) conducted a diary study and asked participants to note down the most stressful event of the day. Based on nearly 10,000 events, 20% were work related. More specifically, 15% of all events (which is 75% of all work-related events), comprised negative emotional interactions with colleagues, supervisors, or clients. In comparison, time pressure occurred in only 2.8% of all cases. Zapf and Frese (1991) compared work-related stressors (time pressure, organizational problems, uncertainty, environmental stressors, and danger of accidents) and social stressors (bad group climate and conflicts with colleagues and supervisors) at work. They found that social stressors were significant but less important than work stressors for psychosomatic complaints and irritation. But they were more important than work stressors for depression and anxiety. Finally, Spector (1987) identified interpersonal stressors to be most important in a sample of university secretaries. Problems of social relationships with clients as another type of social stress has been researched in the burnout literature (e.g. Schaufeli, Maslach, & Marek, 1993). However, this will not be considered here.

In a recent review of longitudinal studies in organizational stress research (Zapf, Dormann, & Frese, 1996) we found only two studies that considered conflicts with colleagues or supervisors as a source of stress. Even less research has been done so far on the severe forms of social stressors at work called mobbing. Ashforth (1994) noted that very negative leadership behaviour (tyrannical behaviours) has seldom been explored, particularly not with respect to ill-health effects on subordinates, probably because research on effective leadership typically implies that ineffective leadership reflects simply the absence of those factors that make leadership effective. This may explain why tyrannical behaviours such as arbitrariness or belittling subordinates has not been explicitly studied. Similarly, communication possibilities at work and social support by colleagues were frequently studied in the past (Kahn & Byosiere, 1992). However, harassing a colleague can certainly not be equated with the absence of support. Mobbing cases published so far (e.g. Adams, 1992; Einarsen, Raknes, Matthiesen, & Hellesøy, 1994; Groeblinghoff & Becker, this issue; Leymann, 1993b) clearly stress that negative social behaviour is more than the absence of positive behaviour and is a research theme in its own right.

As much is said on the definition of mobbing in this issue (Leymann, this issue). We will constrain ourselves in this article to the relationship between social or interpersonal stressors and mobbing.

Mobbing should be understood as a subset of social stressors at work. The basic characteristic of social stressors is that they are related to the social relations of employees within the organization. Relationships to clients are not considered here. Whereas social stressors occur as daily hassles (Kanner, Coyne, Schaefer, & Lazarus, 1981), mobbing occurs on the one hand in the form of daily hassles; on the other hand, there are cases in which mobbing is experienced as a very critical life event, for example, when physical or sexual violence is used. Social stressors may occur more or less often and be more or less frequent. Leymann (1993b) suggested an operational definition of mobbing. To call it "mobbing", such actions should last at least half a year and should occur at least once a week. Social stressors can occur under both equal or unequal power structures and the power structure will usually not change because of the stressors. Frequent minor conflicts may occur between colleagues in a similar position or between supervisor and subordinate, affecting the well-being of all individuals involved in the conflicts. The case studies described in the literature suggest that individuals in a weak power position are more likely to become mobbing victims. This is underscored by several studies in German-speaking countries in which supervisors who are in a more powerful position were among the mobbers in more than 75% of cases (Knorz & Zapf, 1996; Niedl, 1995; Zapf, Renner, Bühler, & Weinl, 1996). However, mobbing can also start with an equal power structure, but for various reasons an unequal power structure will result after some time. There is even a low percentage of cases where supervisors who are at least formally in a superior power position were mobbed by their subordinates. (Leymann, 1993b; Niedl, 1995). The victims are pushed into an inferior position which limits their resources to defend themselves. Also, if social stressors occur in a department, almost everybody will be negatively affected after some time; mobbing, however, is targeted at a particular individual. This individual will show severe health consequences after some time whereas the perpetrators and observers may not be affected at all.

Given all these differences between social stressors and mobbing, the introduction of the term mobbing seems justified to signify this very severe stress situation, which was not well described in the previous stress literature. Neuberger (1995b) pointed out that the phenomenon of mobbing is already well covered in concepts on conflicts and on micropolitics in organizations. Clearly, there is some overlap of the concepts. Among others, conflict literature describes the development and management of conflicts (e.g. Glasl, 1982, 1994; Thomas, 1992) and, thus, also describes essential issues related to mobbing. However, conflict theories do not deal with the health consequences of the individuals involved in conflicts. The same is true for micropolitics (see Neuberger, 1995a). In addition, there are many cases where mobbing is caused by factors which would hardly fall under micropolitic behaviour, for example, in the case of a jealous supervisor harassing his secretary who has terminated their love affair. Thus, there are good reasons to introduce the term mobbing to characterize the situation where a person is harassed by colleagues, supervisors, and sometimes subordinates leading to severe health consequences for this person (see also Leymann, this issue).

RESEARCH QUESTIONS

In this article the key questions are: (1) Is mobbing a homogeneous construct or are there various factors of mobbing? (2) Are these mobbing factors related to variables of job content, the social work environment, and psychological health?

(1) Homogeneity means that all the mobbing actions have similar causes and consequences and occur under the same circumstances. There is some evidence that various facets of mobbing can be differentiated. Ashforth (1987, cited in Ashforth, 1994) developed a questionnaire on tyrannical behaviours and found six different factors: arbitrariness and self-aggrandizement; belittling subordinates; lack of consideration; a forcing style of conflict resolution; discouraging initiative; and noncontingent punishment. Leymann (1986) differentiated between five classes of mobbing behaviour: attacking a person's possibilities of communication; attacking a person's social relationships; attacking a person's social reputation; attacking the quality of a person's occupational and life situation; and attacking a person's health. In an empirical study, Leymann (1992) found factors which he labelled as negative communication, humiliating behaviour, isolating behaviour, frequent changes of tasks to punish someone, and violence or threat of violence. Vartia (1993) found six main forms of mobbing: slander, social isolation, giving a person too few or overly simple tasks, threatening or criticizing, physical violence and threat of violence, and insinuations about the victim's mental health. Factor analyses of the work harassment scale led Björkqvist (1992) to two strategies: the rationale strategy (based on logic and rationale reasoning such as criticizing, interrupting, or wrongly judging someone's work) and social manipulation (spreading rumours). Based on factor analyses of the LIPT questionnaire Niedl (1995) identified seven factors: attacking a person's integrity, isolation, direct and indirect critique, sanction by certain tasks, threats, sexual encroachment, and attacking a person's private sphere. Finally, factor analyses of the negative acts questionnaire (NAQ) led to five factors

(Einarsen & Raknes, 1995), four of which can easily be interpreted as attacking the private person, social isolation, work-related measures, and physical violence. The question is whether in this study these or similar types of mobbing behaviours will be found.

(2) The background of the second question is the public discussion on the reasons for mobbing. It is often argued that it is the fault of the victims themselves when they are harassed because of their socially incompetent behaviour, low achievement, or pathological personalities. Leymann (1993a, 1993b) on the other hand expressed the conviction that the origins of mobbing are not part of the victims' characteristics. He claims that organizational factors, such as bad job content and a bad social environment, are responsible for mobbing. If Leymann's hypothesis is true then mobbing should be negatively correlated with variables such as job complexity, job control and variability, and social support by colleagues and supervisors.

METHOD

Samples

The research questions were studied in two different samples. For the first sample, 50 mobbing victims completed standardized questionnaires, 19 of whom took part in a qualitative interview. Another two took part in the interview, but did not complete the questionnaire (Knorz & Zapf, 1996). Seventy percent were women, aged between 17 and 58 with a mean of 42 years. Eighteen percent of the sample had a higher education degree (Abitur) and 24% had a university degree. For the second sample, quantitative data of 99 mobbing victims were collected. Sixty-one subjects serving as a control group were collected using a snowball system and starting with people who could be directly approached by Kulla (Kulla, Gundlach, & Zapf, 1996). Sixty-five percent of this mobbing sample were women. Age in the mobbing group ranged from 20 to 60 years with a mean of 43 years. Twelve percent had a higher education degree and 23% had a university degree; 57% of the control group were women, age ranged from 21 to 57 with a mean of 32 years; 28% had a higher education degree and 34% a university degree. The mobbing victims in both samples were recruited by means of newspaper articles on mobbing, local broadcasting, and mobbing self-help groups.

It should be noted that the samples were not randomly drawn. This was not possible for the mobbing samples because getting access to mobbing victims was and still is very difficult and we had to be content with this situation. Women are clearly over-represented. We are careful in drawing the conclusion that women are more often mobbing victims than men. This could be a selection effect because women are more open to answering health-related questions than men. However, other studies seem to support the higher victimization rate of women in Germany (Halama & Möckel, 1995; Zapf et al., 1996). Moreover, our analyses on coping with mobbing suggest that individuals with an active approach are over-represented (Knorz & Zapf, 1996; Kulla et al., 1996).

Instruments

Mobbing was measured with the help of a German translation of the Leymann Inventory of Psychological Terrorization (LIPT: Leymann, 1990) taken from Leymann (1993b). The original questionnaire consists of 45 items representing various mobbing actions. We divided the item "attacking a person's political and religious attitudes" into two items. The items had to be answered according to how frequently they appeared (answering scale: "often"—"sometimes"—"never" in sample I; "daily"—"at least once a week"—"at least once a month"—"more seldom"—"never" in sample II). In addition, scales measuring aspects of tasks and the social work environment were used.

Several measures were taken from the Instrument for Stress-oriented Job Analysis (ISTA; Semmer, Zapf, & Dunckel, in press; Zapf, 1995). "Complexity" measures whether a job comprises routine vs. problem-solving tasks. "Control over tasks" is a measure of decision possibilities with regard to the sequence of tasks or subtasks and individual strategies of task fulfilment. "Variability" measures whether one's tasks are all different or similar and whether one can use a variety of tools. "Control over time" comprises decision possibilities with regard to time aspects, e.g. for how long one could leave one's workplace without causing trouble. "Communication possibilities" was taken as a descriptive measure of the number of people to whom one can talk or whom one can help during work. "Co-operation requirements" measures how closely one's work is coupled to the work of others. Because of space reasons not all scales of the ISTA instrument could be used. We constrained ourselves to aspects of job content and collaboration because case studies suggested the relevance of these job characteristics.

A scale of social stressors (Frese & Zapf, 1987) comprised items referring to the social climate in the work group, and conflicts with colleagues and supervisors. A German version of the social support scales developed by Caplan (Caplan, Cobb, French, van Harrison, & Pinneau, 1975) and adapted by Frese (1989) measured social support by colleagues, supervisors, spouse/partner, and friends.

Psychological health was measured with several scales developed by Mohr (1986, 1991). A scale of "irritation" included such items as "being irritated", "nervous", or "cannot stop thinking about work"; a scale of psychosomatic complaints included such items as "how often do you suffer from headaches, high blood pressure, insomnia", etc.; depression was measured with items such as "I feel lonesome, even when together with other people" or "I look forward to the future hopelessly"; self-esteem was measured using cognitive–evaluative aspects in assessing one's self as well as concomitant emotions related to one's self-image—an example item is "I am proud of my achievements".

RESULTS

In order to find substructures of mobbing, exploratory factor analyses were applied in both mobbing samples. The following criteria were used to come up with an acceptable solution: (1) We used the scree-test to receive information on the possible number of factors. This led to five-, six-, and seven-factor solutions in both samples; (2) Similar factors should occur in both samples; (3) Only those items were considered that loaded similarly on the respective factor in both samples; (4) Some items were excluded from a factor because of theoretical considerations.

It should be noted that the factor analyses were applied in an exploratory manner and that conclusions drawn from the factor solution should be drawn with care. The sample sizes compared to the number of variables are very small. Therefore, similarities in both samples and similarities with prior findings were considered to be important in the evaluation of the factors. The factor solution chosen is shown in Table 1.

Altogether, the seven factors comprise 38 out of 45 items of the LIPT. The factors found were similar to Leymann's categorization and Niedl's

TABLE 1
Mobbing Factors: Reliabilities and Item Discrimination Based on Factor Analytical Results of the Two Mobbing Samples

	Cronbach's α and Item Discrimination	
	Sample I	Sample II
1. Attacking the victim with **organizational measures**	α = 0.79	α = 0.86
The supervisor restricts a person's possibilities to speak	0.46	0.56
Moving a person to a room far from his/her colleagues	0.25	0.54
Forbidding his/her colleagues to talk to the person concerned	0.28	0.52
Forcing somebody to carry out tasks affecting his or her self-consciousness	0.61	0.65
Judging a person's job performance wrongly or in an offending manner	0.45	0.50
Questioning a person's decisions	0.34	0.46
Refusal to assign any tasks to the person concerned	0.29	0.58
Removing a person from all occupations so that even the person concerned is at a loss what to do next	0.46	0.53

(Continued)

TABLE 1
(Continued)

	Cronbach's α and Item Discrimination	
	Sample I	Sample II
Assigning senseless tasks to the person concerned	0.57	0.64
Assigning the person concerned tasks far below his/her skills	0.56	0.54
Assigning degrading tasks to the person concerned	0.62	0.63
2. Attacking the victim's **social relationships with social isolation**	α = 0.84	α = 0.83
Colleagues restrict the person's possibilities to speak	0.54	0.38
Refusal to communicate with the person concerned by means of slighting glances and gestures	0.65	0.67
Refusal to communicate with the person concerned by means of dropping hints without speaking out directly	0.58	0.58
One does not talk to the person concerned	0.60	0.73
Refusal to be talked to	0.70	0.71
Being treated like air	0.64	0.56
3. Attacking the victim's **private life**	α = 0.73	α = 0.75
Permanently criticizing a person's private life	0.64	0.52
Telephone terror	0.24	0.35
Making a person look stupid	0.33	0.51
Suspecting a person to be psychologically disturbed	0.56	0.37
Making fun of a person's handicap	0.37	0.39
Imitating a person's gait, voice, or gestures to make him/her look stupid	0.42	0.49
Making fun of a person's private life	0.61	0.68
4. **Physical violence**	α = 0.40	α = 0.69
Forced psychiatric treatment	0.36	0.46
Sexual approaches and sexual offers	0.01	0.60
Threat of physical violence	0.09	0.42
Minor use of violence	0.36	0.21
Physical maltreatment	0.42	0.61
Sexual violence	—[a]	0.62
5. Attacking the victim's **attitudes**	α = 0.52	α = 0.63
Attacking a person's political attitudes	0.21	0.49
Attacking a person's religious attitudes	0.50	0.40
Making fun of a person's nationality	0.37	0.55
6. **Verbal aggression**	α = 0.57	α = 0.66
Shouting at or cursing loudly at a person	0.43	0.53
Permanently criticizing a person's work	0.31	0.45
Verbal threats	0.41	0.44
7. **Rumours**	r = 0.71[b]	r = 0.65[b]
Saying nasty things about a person behind his/her back		
Spreading rumours		

[a]No variance for this item in sample I; [b]Correlation coefficient computed because this scale consists of only two items.

(1995) factor analytical results of the LIPT but not identical. The chosen factor solution comes very close to the results of Vartia (1993) with five factors almost identical. It comes also close to the factor solution of Einarsen and Raknes (1995) with four similar factors. The first factor, "organizational measures" either consists of behaviours initiated by the supervisor or aspects directly related to the victim's tasks. The second factor, "social isolation" is related to informal social relationships at work; an example is the item "colleagues restrict the person's possibilities to speak". The third factor is related to individual attributes of the victim and the victim's private life. The fourth factor, "physical violence", includes two items of sexual harassment as well as general physical violence or threat of violence. The fifth factor, "attacking the victim's attitudes" is related to political, national, and religious attitudes. The factor "verbal aggression" consists of items related to verbal attacks. Finally, there was a factor consisting of two items related to spreading rumours.

The respective items for each mobbing factor were summed up and divided by the number of items to create the mobbing factors which were used in the further analyses of this article. Table 1 also shows Cronbach's alpha as a measure of the reliability of the scales and the item discrimination scores. The reliability measures should be used with care, because for theoretical reasons one cannot expect that all mobbing behaviours of a factor occur together. This is particularly so in the case of the factors "violence" and "attacking attitudes"; for example, a person who experiences threats of violence needs not necessarily have problems with sexual harassment. Nevertheless it can be useful to sum up these variables because they behave similarly when related to other variables and they build up one theoretical construct namely, for example, physical violence. There may be, of course, occasions where it makes more sense to treat sexual harassment separately from other violent behaviour.

Table 2 shows the correlations of the mobbing factors. One would, of course, expect positive correlations between the mobbing factors because there is no evidence in the literature that mobbing is restricted to a very specific kind of mobbing (for example, a person is only mobbed by social isolation). Rather, reading the case studies one would expect that, on average, several types of mobbing occur at the same time, thus leading to positive correlations between the mobbing factors. On the other hand, the correlations should not be too high, because this would question the discriminant validity of the mobbing factors. Very high correlations of the mobbing factors would suggest that there is either mobbing or not. Table 2 shows that there are several significant correlations of the mobbing factors. In particular, there were substantial correlations between "organizational measures", "social isolation", "attacking the private person", "verbal aggression", and "rumours". "Attacking attitudes" and "physical violence" showed low correlations on average. Correlations regarding these factors

TABLE 2
Correlations of Mobbing Factors

	Organizational Measures	Social Isolation	Attacking Private Person	Attacking Attitudes	Physical Violence	Verbal Aggression	Rumours
Organizational measures		0.46**	0.12	0.09	0.11	0.40**	0.48**
Social isolation	0.40** (0.46**)		0.25	0.25	0.14	0.34*	0.33*
Attacking private person	0.29** (0.44**)	0.41** (0.72**)		0.14	0.16	0.39**	0.37**
Attacking attitudes	0.07 (0.34**)	0.15 (0.52**)	0.06 (0.70**)		0.45**	0.24	0.18
Physical violence	0.15 (0.11)	0.17 (0.07)	0.31** (0.09)	0.17 (0.11)		0.08	0.18
Verbal aggression	0.35** (0.52**)	0.27** (0.72**)	0.36** (0.67**)	0.10 (0.56**)	0.29** (0.23)		0.43**
Rumours	0.37** (0.35**)	0.52** (0.47**)	0.44** (0.47**)	0.00 (0.26*)	0.20* (0.10)	0.26** (0.44**)	

*$P < 0.05$; **$P < 0.01$; Upper triangle: Mobbing sample I: $N = 50$; Lower triangle: Mobbing sample II: $N = 99$; in parentheses: control group: $N = 61$.

were small because of their low variances. There was only one correlation in the two mobbing samples which was higher than $r = 0.50$. In the control sample, there were seven out of 21 correlations higher than $r = 0.50$. All in all, this should be regarded as sufficient evidence for the discriminant validity of the mobbing factors.

The next question was: Do mobbing and control group of sample II differ with respect to all mobbing factors? This analysis is shown in Table 3.

Mobbing victims and control group could indeed be differentiated in all mobbing factors. As can be seen from the t-values, there were considerable differences between the groups. The smallest differences occurred for "physical violence" and "attacking the person's attitudes". These mobbing behaviours hardly occurred in either samples. Rumours occurred in both groups most often. As in the study of Vartia (1993), social isolation was also very frequent.

Mobbing and Job Content

In the next analysis the job content variables of the mobbing samples was compared to the control group of sample II and two other samples of metal workers (Greif, Bamberg, & Semmer, 1991) and office employees (Zapf, 1993), where the same instruments were used.

Because not all measures were available not all analyses could be done in both samples. Table 4 shows that the mobbing sample I had higher complexity and variability compared with the sample of office employees. Control over tasks was higher than in the metal worker and office employees sample but not as high as in the control group of the second study. However, control over time was significantly lower than in the office employee group. The control group of the second sample showed the highest mean control over tasks.

TABLE 3
Mobbing Scores of Mobbing and Control Group in Sample II

	Mobbing (N = 99)		Control (N = 61)		
	Mean	SD	Mean	SD	t
Organizational measures	1.30	0.95	0.33	0.36	9.20**
Social isolation	2.16	1.14	0.45	0.72	11.56**
Attacking private life	0.88	0.77	0.13	0.34	8.41**
Attacking attitudes	0.26	0.51	0.13	0.31	2.01*
Physical violence	0.14	0.32	0.05	0.12	2.46*
Verbal aggression	1.68	0.99	0.48	0.76	8.64**
Rumours	2.46	1.32	0.57	0.94	10.57**

*$P < 0.05$; **$P < 0.01$; Scale score = mean score of the respective items; Range of the scales between 0 and 4.

TABLE 4

Comparison of Job Content, the Social Work Situation, and Mental Health Variables of the Two Mobbing Samples, the Control Sample, and Two Other Samples of Metal Workers (Greif et al., 1991) and Office Employees (Zapf, 1993)

Scales	Cronbach α[a]	Number of Items	Range	Mobbing Sample I		Mobbing Sample II		Control Sample Mean	Greif et al. (1991) Mean	Zapf (1993) Mean
				Mean	SD	Mean	SD			
Job complexity	0.73	4	1-5	2.99	1.05	-	-	-	-	2.98
Control over tasks	0.89 (0.93)	6	1-5	3.18	1.01	3.18	1.14	3.96*	2.84*	2.85*
Variability	0.25	2	1-5	2.79	1.03	-	-	-	2.88	3.08
Control over time	0.69	4	1-5	3.37	1.16	-	-	-	-	3.92*
Communication possibilities	0.41	3	1-5	3.37	0.90	-	-	-	3.24	-
Co-operation requirements	0.80	5	1-5	2.59	1.15	-	-	-	2.04**	-
Social stressors	0.73 (0.75)	8	1-4	2.53	0.62	2.63	0.65	1.78**	1.96**	1.54**
Social support/supervisor	0.81	4	1-4	1.63	0.62	-	-	-	2.72**	-
Social support/colleagues	0.83	4	1-4	1.97	0.58	-	-	-	2.68**	-
Psychosomatic complaints	0.91 (0.93)	20	1-5	3.50	0.74	3.24	0.92	2.21**	2.27**	2.10**
Irritation	0.86 (0.87)	8	1-7	5.11	1.08	4.66	1.33	3.12**	3.30**	2.71**
Depression	0.88	9	1-7	3.66	1.15	-	-	-	2.71**	-
Self-esteem	0.81	8	1-5	3.95	0.37	-	-	-	4.18**	-

*$P < 0.05$; **$P < 0.01$; Significances in the columns of the control group, metal worker, and office employee sample indicate differences referring to both mobbing samples; – indicates that the measure was not available in the sample; [a]alphas of mobbing sample I without parentheses and mobbing sample II in parentheses.

Relationships between mobbing factors and job content variables are shown in Table 5. The overall picture of the correlations between mobbing factors and job contents variables is that all significant correlations between mobbing and job content variables were negative suggesting that more intensive mobbing goes along with worse job content. Within the mobbing victims, the most consistent pattern of negative correlations occurred with verbal aggression. Organizational measures showed negative correlations with control over tasks, job complexity, and variability in sample I.

Mobbing and the Social Situation at Work

Table 4 shows no differences between the mobbing samples and the control groups in communication possibilities. There were higher co-operation requirements for the mobbing sample I in comparison with the metal worker sample. In both mobbing samples, clearly more social stressors were reported in comparison with the other samples. Moreover, in the mobbing sample I, less social support from supervisors and colleagues was reported in comparison with the metal worker sample. All reported differences were substantial. These results correspond to Einarsen, Raknes, and Matthiesen (1994) who found negative correlations between mobbing and satisfaction with social climate and leadership.

Relationships between mobbing factors and variables of the social work environment are shown in Table 5. For the total sample II, there were six significant correlations out of seven with social stressors. That is, a general measure of social stressors goes along with most of the mobbing factors. For the low correlations of "attacking attitudes" and "physical violence", the low variance of these variables must again be taken into consideration. Within the mobbing samples, significant correlations turned up for "verbal aggression" and "rumours". Somewhat lower correlations occurred for "organizational measures" and "attacking the private person". In the mobbing sample I, higher communication possibilities were correlated with less "attacking the private person" and "verbal aggression". High co-operation requirements were correlated with lower "social isolation".

Mobbing with "organizational measures" was correlated with both social support factors; social isolation and attacking the private person were negatively correlated with support by colleagues, but not with support by the supervisor. In contrast, verbal aggression was negatively correlated with social support by the supervisor, but not with support by colleagues.

Mobbing and Mental Health

In the next analysis the mental health of the mobbing samples was compared to the control group and the two other samples (Table 4). Little comment is necessary for these findings. The results were very much in line with those

TABLE 5

Correlations between Mobbing Factors and Job Content Variables and Social Characteristics at Work

	Organizational Measures	Social Isolation	Attacking Private Person	Attacking Attitudes	Physical Violence	Verbal Aggression	Rumours
Mobbing Sample I Control Over Tasks ($N = 50$)	-0.24	-0.25	-0.06	0.17	0.18	-0.25	-0.23
Mobbing Sample II Control Over Tasks ($N = 94$)	-0.02	-0.14	-0.11	-0.04	-0.09	-0.25**	-0.03
Total Sample II Control Over Tasks ($N = 160$)	-0.24**	-0.34**	-0.28**	-0.10	-0.12	-0.38**	-0.22**
Mobbing Sample I							
Job Complexity	-0.28*	-0.31*	0.06	0.07	0.21	-0.25*	0.00
Variability	-0.27	-0.12	-0.02	0.16	0.25	-0.37**	-0.10
Control Over Time	0.04	-0.15	-0.12	0.07	0.20	-0.25*	-0.08
Mobbing Sample I Social Stressors ($N = 50$)	0.30*	0.01	0.14	0.10	-0.10	0.47**	0.32*
Mobbing Sample II Social Stressors ($N = 94$)	0.15	0.00	0.23*	0.01	0.09	0.35**	0.19
Total Sample II Social Stressors ($N = 160$)	0.41**	0.40**	0.43**	0.09	0.16*	0.53**	0.48**
Mobbing Sample I							
Communication Possibilities	-0.11	-0.11	-0.25	-0.09	-0.02	-0.38**	-0.09
Co-operation Requirements	-0.11	-0.26	-0.02	-0.19	-0.25	-0.02	-0.12
Social Support/Supervisor	-0.42**	-0.16	-0.03	-0.18	-0.14	-0.41**	-0.41**
Social Support/Colleagues	-0.35**	-0.46**	-0.28*	-0.18	-0.22	-0.17	-0.30*

*$P < 0.05$; **$P < 0.01$.

of Niedl (1995), who used the same instruments in his study. All mental health variables showed highly significant differences between the mobbing samples and the others. Psychosomatic complaints showed notable differences of about two standard deviations. Thus, the results confirm findings of Leymann (1993b, this issue) and many case studies reporting the severe health consequences of mobbing. The next question was again: How were the mobbing factors related to psychological health? This can be seen in Table 6.

For the total sample, high correlations were found for "organizational measures", "social isolation", "attacking the private person", "verbal aggression", and "rumours. Within the mobbing samples, "attacking the private person" showed the most consistent correlations with the health variables. These results were confirmed in multiple regressions with the health variables as dependent variables and with the mobbing factors as independent variables. In most cases, "attacking the private person" was the only predictor with a significant beta weight. This result suggests that the victims' health was in a particularly bad shape when their private life was under attack. It corresponds to results of Einarsen and Raknes (1995) who found the highest correlation between a similar mobbing factor and a scale on psychological health and well-being.

DISCUSSION

In the following we discuss the most important findings of this study. Factor analyses led to seven factors of mobbing. Four of these mobbing factors, "organizational measures", "social isolation", "attacking the private person", and "physical violence" could also be found in most of the other empirical studies (Einarsen & Raknes, 1995; Leymann, 1992; Niedl, 1995; Vartia, 1993). "Verbal aggression" also appeared in Vartia's (1993) study and "rumours" occurred as a factor in Björkqvist's (1992) study. Only "attacking the victim's attitudes" occurred in the present study as a separate factor. However, the frequency of "attacking attitudes" in the present samples was very low. The present results do not differ much from the results of the other studies in this respect.

The means of the mobbing factors in the mobbing group were all significantly higher than the means of the control group. The smallest differences occurred for "physical violence" and "attacking attitudes", which was explained by the low frequency of these behaviours in both the mobbing and the control group. Taking these findings together it appears that "organizational measures", "social isolation", "attacking the private person", "verbal aggression", and "spreading rumours" are typical strategies of mobbing whereas "attacking attitudes" and "physical violence" occur only occasionally in the context of mobbing. Thus, the results underline that

TABLE 6
Correlations and Multiple Regressions between Mobbing Factors and Mental Health

	Psychosomatic Complaints			Irritation			Depression	Self-esteem
	Mobbing Sample I (N = 50)	Mobbing Sample II (N = 94)	Sample II Total (N = 152)	Mobbing Sample I (N = 50)	Mobbing Sample II (N = 96)	Sample II Total (N = 156)	Mobbing Sample I (N = 50)	Mobbing Sample I (N = 50)
Correlations								
Organizational measures	0.14	0.16	0.43**	0.10	0.08	0.37**	0.01	0.10
Social isolation	0.10	0.18	0.50**	-0.14	0.12	0.48**	0.07	0.00
Attacking private person	0.56**	0.26*	0.47**	0.30*	0.25**	0.44**	0.42**	-0.26
Attacking attitudes	0.09	-0.10	0.01	-0.15	-0.05	0.04	0.08	0.03
Physical violence	0.00	-0.01	0.08	-0.06	0.16	0.20**	0.14	0.13
Verbal aggression	0.18	0.09	0.41**	0.11	0.20*	0.45**	0.24	-0.20
Rumours	0.21	0.08	0.43**	0.24	0.11	0.39**	0.16	0.05
Multiple regressions (betas)								
Organizational measures	0.15	0.10	0.12	0.13	-0.03	0.01	-0.08	0.12
Social isolation	-0.09	0.14	0.25*	-0.30	0.05	0.28**	-0.04	0.02
Attacking private person	0.62**	0.25*	0.22*	0.32*	0.17	0.13	0.37*	-0.27
Attacking attitudes	0.09	-0.12	-0.11	-0.14	-0.10	-0.11	-0.03	0.02
Physical violence	-0.13	-0.08	-0.09	-0.05	0.09	0.06	0.10	0.14
Verbal aggression	-0.09	-0.01	0.12	-0.01	0.13	0.22*	0.14	-0.23
Rumours	-0.01	-0.12	0.02	0.21	-0.02	0.00	0.00	0.16
R	0.59**	0.33	0.57**	0.48	0.30	0.55**	0.44	0.40
adj. R^2	0.24	0.04	0.30	0.10	0.02	0.27	0.06	0.02

*$P < 0.05$; **$P < 0.01$.

mobbing is primarily to do with psychological and not with physical violence. This is in line with Leymann (this issue) who suggested that there is a difference between mobbing at work and bullying at school where physical violence is in the foreground (Olweus, 1993).

"Rumours" occurred most often followed by "social isolation" and "verbal aggression" (cf. Table 3); next frequent were the "organizational measures"; less frequent were "attacking the victim's private life", "attitudes", and, least frequent, "physical violence". Identical results appeared in both samples in this respect. It would be interesting to see whether the more seldom mobbing behaviours occur at later stages in the mobbing process and at a higher level of conflict escalation (Glasl, 1982).

It should be mentioned that one cannot draw the conclusion from these data that xenophobia or sexual harassment is not a problem in German firms. The present study did not aim at these behaviours. Therefore, their general frequencies are certainly underestimated (see, for example, Holzbecher, 1992 or Rastetter, 1994 for the frequency of sexual harassment in German firms).

Mobbed subjects had jobs with good or average job complexity and task control, but they had less control over time than a sample of office employees. The interpretation of these results is first that mobbing is a problem primarily of employees working in public administration, health services, schools, and offices in general and less a problem of industrial workers whose jobs are typically characterized by low complexity and control. In addition there is little evidence for "mobbing because of boredom" (Leymann, 1993b) as a frequent phenomenon (given that the jobs of the mobbers are similar to those of the victims) although such cases appear occasionally. It is interesting, however, that mobbing victims had less control over time than the other groups. Conflict management is time consuming. If little time is available to solve arising conflicts because of restricted control over time, then there is an increased likelihood that unsolved conflicts escalate at a later point in time. Leymann (this issue) suggested that this is a typical trigger for a mobbing process.

The mobbing victims had higher co-operation requirements. It is known from previous analyses that co-operation requirements must be interpreted as being dependent on colleagues in a negative sense, i.e. being forced to work together (Semmer, 1984). It is likely that being forced to collaborate offers more possibilities for unresolved conflicts as a basis for mobbing behaviour to emerge. This hypothesis received some support by case reports (Knorz, 1994). High co-operation requirements showed a weak correlation with low social isolation. This makes sense: If somebody's tasks make co-operation necessary, it is more difficult to isolate this person. High co-operation requirements are a plausible source of latent conflicts. These latent conflicts can trigger a mobbing process. However, if a group is very closely coupled by the co-operation requirements the strategy to isolate a certain person is difficult to apply. Other strategies such as "organizational measures", "verbal aggression", or "attacking the private person" are probably more likely in such cases. The present data and design are too weak to draw strong conclusions in this respect. However, this seems to be an interesting hypothesis which should be analysed in future studies, particularly because group work where co-operation requirements are high is an increasing phenomenon in many countries (Antoni, 1994; Ulich, 1994).

Also interesting are the relationships between the social stressors scale and the mobbing factors. With regard to the total sample II including both the mobbing and the control sample, there were substantial correlations between social stressors and "organizational measures", "social isolation", "attacking the private person", "verbal aggression", and "rumours", with the highest correlation between social stressors and "verbal aggression" and "rumours". The connotation of verbal aggression and talking badly about other people is actually what we had in mind when we developed the social stressors scale (Frese & Zapf, 1987). It is obvious that social stressor or personal conflict scales used in stress research only partly measure (milder) forms of mobbing. In particular social isolation is something which is not covered by the social stressors scale. This is shown by the zero-correlations between social stressors and social isolation in the mobbing samples. The correlation of $r = 0.40$ in the total sample II including the mobbing sample and the control group can be explained by the correlations of the mobbing factors. We tested this using multiple regression of social stressors on the mobbing factors. Only verbal aggression and rumour had a significant beta weight. We, therefore, think that social isolation is an important but so far little considered social stressor which was uncovered in mobbing research but which is probably also relevant in the wider context of stress research.

It is certainly not surprising that the mobbing victims report lower social support than the other samples. It is, however, interesting that the support scales are differentially correlated with the mobbing factors. Mobbing with "organizational measures" was correlated with both support factors, although it was primarily the supervisors who used such measures (see the higher correlation). Supervisors have, of course, the formal power to use most of the organizational mobbing behaviours, whereas colleagues can usually only use informal power. Social support by colleagues shows the negative correlations with social isolation and attacking the private person which is not the case for social support by supervisors. Such isolation is certainly a strategy which can only be applied when the colleagues are involved. Otherwise this strategy would not work. A supervisor alone cannot isolate a subordinate. Although a supervisor can try to "order" the isolation, this can only be put into practice if the colleagues lack interest to support the victim. The correlational pattern also suggests that attacking the private life is a preferred strategy of colleagues and less of supervisors. A reason for this may be that this mobbing strategy requires information about the victim's private life which is probably less available for the supervisors. Finally, verbal aggression seems to be more often used by supervisors than by colleagues which may have its reason in the power structure of supervisors and subordinates.

Dramatic differences in health variables between the mobbing samples and all other samples were found. If the results are, for example, compared to those of Niedl (1995) the higher scores may reflect the selection procedures of the present samples which may have led to a sample of more severe cases. As demonstrated by the analyses of Leymann and Gustafsson (this issue) the health of a sample of mobbing victims is comparable to clinical samples. Many of the participants in our studies received medical treatment (54% of sample I; Knorz, 1994). More than 55% of sample I had three or more periods of sick leave during the previous 12 months (Knorz, 1994) compared to 20% of the sample of metal workers (Mohr, 1986). Twenty-four percent said that they used long-term sick leaves as a strategy to cope with mobbing (Knorz & Zapf, 1996). Within the mobbing samples, "attacking the private person" showed the most consistent correlations with the health variables. That is, the mobbing victims in the worst health state were those whose private sphere was under attack. The huge scale of ill-health in both samples underscores that mobbing is indeed an extreme form of social stressors which is hardly being dealt with.

In sum, the results show that mobbing leads to severe health consequences and that mobbing is related to job content and social work environment variables. There is some indication that organizational factors can be made responsible for the occurrence of mobbing. However, several alternative mechanisms would explain such data. First, because the data are based on self-reports only, the results may be caused by method effects such as social desirability or negative affectivity (e.g. Spector & Brannick, 1995). However, such method effects usually lead to distortions for all variables in the same direction. More differentiated patterns of correlations as in the present paper (e.g. the relationship between social support variables and mobbing) are difficult to explain by such mechanisms. Rather, one would expect uniform results for all mobbing factors. Moreover, Einarsen, Raknes, & Matthiesen (1994) found that individuals who observed others to be victims, but were not victims or mobbers themselves, reported less satisfaction with work-control, social climate, leadership, and role conflict compared to those who did not observe mobbing. Such results would also be difficult to be explained by mechanisms such as social desirability. Another explanation is that mobbing is caused by the victim's personality (cf. the drift hypothesis, Frese, 1982). Personality variables affect job content or social work environment variables either directly or indirectly by the mobbing process. Integrating into a work group and asking for social support in a socially acceptable manner requires social competencies which may not be available for potential mobbing victims. Consequently they receive less social support. In this case, the causal chain is from personality traits or social competencies to social work environment variables. Such mechanisms cannot be excluded and should be investigated. It remains to be seen whether they alone can be made responsible for the relationships found in this article.

Yet, another explanation is that mobbing depends on certain characteristics of the mobbers. That is, no matter what the social climate or culture of an organization is, there will always be people who tend to harass others. Little is known about the culprits of mobbing. Both quantitative and case studies suggest that there are cases in which mobbing replaces organizational measures which cannot be carried out otherwise on a legitimate basis. However, it is, of course, very difficult to study the mobbing culprits, for social desirability and impression management reasons. However, we succeeded in investigating communication structures of mobbers for less severe cases of mobbing (milder forms of social isolation and spreading rumours; Krum, 1995). From this study we know that the mobbers are often not aware of what they are doing because they receive little information about the consequences of their behaviour (see also Leymann, 1993b). It cannot be excluded that there are some cases of psychopaths among the mobbers. Babiak (1995) described the case of a psychopathic person who used means which could be classified as mobbing by organizational measures, verbal aggression, spreading rumours, and attacking the victim's private life. Again, we believe that the personalities of the mobbers may contribute to the relationships found in this article but they will probably not be the only cause. In all, there are certainly more open questions than satisfactory answers.

ACKNOWLEDGEMENTS

An earlier version of this article was presented at the symposium "Mobbing—Psychological Terror at Work" at the Seventh European Congress of Work and Organizational Psychology, Györ, Hungary, 19–22 April, 1995. We would like to thank H. Peter Dachler, Hanspeter Irmer, and Heinz Leymann for their helpful comments on an earlier draft of this article.

REFERENCES

Adams, A. (1992). *Bullying at work: How to confront and overcome it.* London: Virago Press.
Antoni, C.H. (1994). Gruppenarbeit—mehr als ein Konzept. Darstellung und Vergleich unterschiedlicher Formen der Gruppenarbeit [Group work—more than a concept: Description and comparison of various forms of group work]. In C. Antoni (Ed.), *Gruppenarbeit in Unternehmen* (pp. 19–48). Weinheim: Psychologie Verlags Union.

Ashforth, B.E. (1987). *Organizations and the petty tyrant: An exploratory study.* Paper presented at the annual meeting of the Academy of Management, New Orleans, Louisiana.

Ashforth, B.E. (1994). Petty tyranny in organizations. *Human Relations, 47,* 755–778.

Babiak, P. (1995). When psychopaths go to work: A case study of an industrial psychopath. *Applied Psychology: An International Review, 44,* 171–188.

Björkqvist, K. (1992). Trakassering förekommer bland anställda vid ÅA. *Meddelanden från Åbo Akademi, 9,* 14–17.

Caplan, R.D., Cobb, S., French, J.R.P., van Harrison, R., & Pinneau, S.R. (1975). *Job demands and worker health.* Washington: National Institute for Occupational Safety and Health (NIOSH).

Cohen, S., & Wills, T.A. (1985). Stress, social support, and the buffering hypothesis. *Psychological Bulletin, 98,* 310–357.

Dohrenwend, B.S., & Dohrenwend, B.P. (Eds.). (1974). *Stressful life events: Their nature and effects.* New York: Wiley.

Einarsen, S., & Raknes, B.I. (1995, April). *Harassment in the workplace and the victimization of men.* Paper presented as a poster at the Seventh European Congress of Work and Organizational Psychology, Györ, Hungary.

Einarsen, S., Raknes, B.I., & Matthiesen, S.B. (1994). Bullying and harassment at work and its relationship with work environment quality: An exploratory study. *The European Work and Organizational Psychologist, 4*(4), 381–401.

Einarsen, S., Raknes, B.I., Matthiesen, S.B., & Hellesøy, O.H. (1994). *Mobbing og harde personkonflikter. Helsefarlig samspill på arbeidsplassen [Bullying and personified conflicts: Health-endangering interaction at work].* Søreidgrend: Sigma Forlag.

Frese, M. (1982). Occupational socialisation and psychological development: An underemphasized research perspective in industrial psychology. *Journal of Occupational Psychology, 55,* 209–224.

Frese, M. (1989). Gütekriterien der Operationalisierung von sozialer Unterstützung am Arbeitsplatz [Psychometric criteria of the operationalization of social support at work]. *Zeitschrift für Arbeitswissenschaft, 43,* 112–122.

Frese, M., & Zapf, D. (1987). Eine Skala zur Erfassung von Sozialen Stressoren am Arbeitsplatz [A scale measuring social stressors at work]. *Zeitschrift für Arbeitswissenschaft, 41,* 134–141.

Glasl, F. (1982). The process of conflict escalation and roles of third parties. In G.B.J. Bomers & R. Peterson (Eds.), *Conflict management and industrial relations* (pp. 119–140). Boston: Kluwer-Nijhoff.

Glasl, F. (1994). *Konfliktmanagement. Ein Handbuch für Führungskräfte und Berater [Conflict management: A handbook for managers and councellors]* (4th ed.). Bern: Verlag Paul Haupt.

Greif, S., Bamberg, E., & Semmer, N. (Eds.). (1991). *Psychischer Streß am Arbeitsplatz [Psychological stress at work].* Göttingen: Hogrefe.

Halama, P., & Möckel, U. (1995). "Mobbing". Acht Beiträge zum Thema Psychoterror am Arbeitsplatz ["Mobbing"—Eight contributions to the subject of psychological terror at work]. In Evangelischer Pressedienst (Ed.), *epd-Dokumentation* (Vol. 11/95). Frankfurt a.M.: Gemeinschaftswerk der Evangelischen Publizistik.

Holzbecher. M. (1992). Sexuelle Belästigung am Arbeitsplatz. Ergebnisse und Auswertung einer bundesweiten Studie [Sexual harassment at work: Results and analysis of a nationwide study]. In U. Gerhart, A. Heiliger, & A. Stehr (Eds.), *Tatort Arbeitsplatz. Sexuelle Belästigung von Frauen* (pp. 22–38). München: Verlag Frauenoffensive.

Kahn, R.L., & Byosiere, P. (1992). Stress in organizations. In M.D. Dunnette & L.M. Hough (Eds.), *Handbook of industrial and organizational psychology* (Vol. 3, pp. 571–650, 2nd ed.). Palo Alto, CA: Consulting Psychologists Press.

Kanner, A.D., Coyne, J.C., Schaefer, C., & Lazarus, R.S. (1981). Comparison of two modes of stress measurement: Daily hassles and uplifts versus major life events. *Journal of Behavioral Medicine, 4*, 1–39.

Knorz, C. (1994). *Mobbing—eine Extremform von sozialem Streß am Arbeitsplatz [Mobbing—an extreme form of social stress at work]*. Unpublished diploma thesis. Department of Psychology, University of Giessen.

Knorz, C., & Zapf, D. (1996). Mobbing—eine extreme Form sozialer Stressoren am Arbeitsplatz [Mobbing—an extreme form of social stressors at work]. *Zeitschrift für Arbeits- und Organisationspsychologie, 40*, 12–21.

Krum, H. (1995). *Mobbing—eine unethische Form der Kommunikations am Arbeitsplatz [Mobbing—an unethical form of communication at work]*. Unpublished diploma thesis. Technical University of Darmstadt.

Kulla, M., Gundlach, G., & Zapf, D. (1996). *Die Bewältigung von Mobbing am Arbeitsplatz. Eine empirische Studie [Coping with mobbing at work: An empirical study]*. Unpublished manuscript. Fakultät für Psychologie und Sportwissenschaft, Universität Bielefeld.

Lazarus, R.S., & Folkman, S. (1984). *Stress, appraisal and coping*. New York: Springer.

Leymann, H. (1986). *Vuxenmobbning—om psykiskt våld i arbetslivet [Mobbing—psychological violence at work places]*. Lund: Studentlitteratur.

Leymann, H. (1990). *Presentation av LIPT-formuläret. Konstruktion, validering, utfall*. Stockholm: Violen inom Praktikertjänst.

Leymann, H. (1992). *Från mobbning til utslagning i arbetslivet [From bullying to exclusion from working life]*. Stockholm: Publica.

Leymann, H. (1993a). Ätiologie und Häufigkeit von Mobbing am Arbeitsplatz—eine Übersicht über die bisherige Forschung [Etiology and frequency of mobbing at work—a research review]. *Zeitschrift für Personalforschung, 7*, 271–283.

Leymann, H. (1993b) *Mobbing—Psychoterror am Arbeitsplatz und wie man sich dagegen wehren kann [Mobbing—psychoterror at work and how one can defend oneself]*. Reinbeck: Rowohlt.

Leymann, H. (1995). Einführung: Mobbing. Das Konzept und seine Resonanz in Deutschland [Introduction: Mobbing. The concept and its resonance in Germany]. In H. Leymann (Ed.), *Der neue Mobbingbericht. Erfahrungen und Initiativen, Auswege und Hilfsangebote* (pp. 13–26). Reinbeck bei Hamburg: Rowohlt.

Mohr, G. (1986). *Die Erfassung psychischer Befindensbeeinträchtigungen bei Arbeitern [The measurement of psychological dysfunctioning of workers]*. Frankfurt a.M.: Peter Lang.

Mohr, G. (1991). Fünf Subkonstrukte psychischer Befindensbeeinträchtigungen bei Industriearbeitern: Auswahl und Entwicklung [Five subconstructs of psychological dysfunctioning of industrial workers: Selection and development]. In S. Greif, E. Bamberg, & N. Semmer (Eds.), *Psychischer Streß am Arbeitsplatz* (pp. 91–119). Göttingen: Hogrefe.

Neuberger, O. (1995a). *Mikropolitik. Der alltägliche Aufbau und Einsatz von Macht in Organisationen [Micropolitics: The ordinary erection and use of power in organizations]*. Stuttgart: Enke.

Neuberger, O. (1995b). *Mobbing. Übel mitspielen in Organisationen [Mobbing—unfair play with people in organizations]*. (2nd ed.). München: Rainer Hampp Verlag.

Niedl, K. (1995). *Mobbing/Bullying am Arbeitsplatz. Eine empirische Analyse zum Phänomen sowie zu personalwirtschaftlich relevanten Effekten von systematischen Feindseligkeiten [Mobbing/bullying at work: An empirical analysis of the phenomenon and of the effects of systematic hostilities relevant for human resource issues]*. München: Rainer Hampp Verlag.

Olweus, D. (1993). *Bullying at school: What we know and what we can do*. Oxford: Blackwell.

Rastetter, D. (1994). *Sexualität und Herrschaft in Organisationen [Sexuality and power in organisations]*. Opladen: Westdeutscher Verlag.

Resch, M. (1994). *Wenn Arbeit krank macht [When work makes ill]*. Frankfurt/Main: Ullstein-Verlag.

Schaufeli, W.B., Maslach, C., & Marek, T. (Eds.). (1993). *Professional burnout: Recent developments in theory and research.* New York: Taylor & Francis.

Schwartz, J.E., & Stone, A.A. (1993). Coping with daily work problems: Contributions of problem content, appraisals, and person factors. *Work and Stress, 7,* 47–62.

Semmer, N. (1984). *Streßbezogene Tätigkeitsanalyse [Stress-oriented job analysis].* Weinheim und Basel: Beltz.

Semmer, N., Zapf, D., & Dunckel, H. (1995). Assessing stress at work: A framework and an instrument. In O. Svane & C. Johansen (Eds.), *Work and health—scientific basis of progress in the working environment* (pp. 105–113). Luxembourg: Office for Official Publications of the European Communities.

Spector, P.E. (1987). Interactive effects of perceived control and job stressors on affective reactions and health outcomes for clerical workers. *Work and Stress, 1,* 155–162.

Spector, P.E., & Brannick, M.T. (1995). The nature and effects of method variance in organizational research. In C.L. Cooper & I.T. Robertson (Eds.), *International review of industrial and organizational psychology* (Vol. 10, pp. 249–274). New York: Wiley.

Thomas, K.W. (1992). Conflict and negotiation processes in organizations. In M.D. Dunnette & L.M. Hough (Eds.), *Handbook of industrial and organizational psychology* (Vol. 3, pp. 651–718). Palo Alto, CA: Consulting Psychologists Press.

Ulich, E. (1994). *Arbeitspsychologie [Work psychology]* (3rd ed.). Stuttgart: Pöschl.

Vartia, M. (1993). Psychological harassment (bullying, mobbing) at work. In K. Kauppinen-Toropainen (Ed.), *OECD Panel group on women, work, and health* (pp. 149–152). Helsinki: Ministry of Social Affairs and Health.

Zapf, D. (1993). Stress-oriented job analysis of computerized office work. *The European Work and Organizational Psychologist, 3*(2), 85–100.

Zapf, D., Dormann, C., & Frese, M. (1996). Longitudinal studies in organizational stress research: A review of the literature with reference to methodological issues. *Journal of Occupational Health Psychology, 1*(2), 145–169.

Zapf, D., & Frese, M. (1991). Soziale Stressoren am Arbeitsplatz und psychische Gesundheit [Social stressors at work and psychological health]. In S. Greif, E. Bamberg, & N. Semmer (Eds.), *Psychischer Streß am Arbeitsplatz* (pp. 168–184). Göttingen: Hogrefe.

Zapf, D., Renner, B., Bühler, K., & Weinl, E. (1996, February). *Sechs Monate Mobbing-telefon in Stuttgart: Eine Evaluation [Six months of the mobbing telephone hotline in Stuttgart: An evaluation].* Paper presented at the conference of the Society against Psychological Stress and Mobbing, Zurich.

EUROPEAN JOURNAL OF WORK AND ORGANIZATIONAL PSYCHOLOGY, 1996, 5 (2), 239–249

Mobbing and Well-being: Economic and Personnel Development Implications[1]

Klaus Niedl

Institute of Human Resource Management, University of Business Administration and Economics, Vienna, Austria

The aim of the study is to investigate the relationship between mobbing at work and the well-being of the affected person, and to explore possible organizational effects of mobbing in connection with coping behaviour. The article reports data from two studies carried out in Austria (368 health professionals) and Germany (10 in-patients) between 1993 and 1994. The results support other findings that mobbing has a negative impact on the well-being of the affected person. Moreover, the results indicate that employees do not cope with mobbing by using simple flight or fight reactions (e.g. absenteeism, lower level of productivity). The results suggest that it should be possible to identify mobbing in an early stage, which, in turn, should enhance the prevention of mobbing.

While different content and context factors of work play an important role in stress analysis, only a small number of authors have focused on stress resulting from negative social interaction at work (see, for example, Bolger, DeLongis, Kessler, & Schilling, 1989; Kahn, 1973; Zapf & Frese, 1991). One reason for this may be seen in the opinion of some researchers that social interactions are influenced by random and situational factors (see, for example, Mergner, 1989) and are, thus, less relevant for organizational and job redesign.

An extreme form of social stressors is mobbing. Although there has been a great deal of research in Scandinavia (e.g. in Norway: Matthiesen, Raknes, & Røkkum, 1989; Skogstad, Matthiesen, & Hellesøy, 1990; in Sweden: Leymann, 1991a; Leymann & Gustavsson, 1984; in Finland: Björkqvist, Österman, & Hjelt-Bäck, 1994; Paanen & Vartia, 1991; Papaioannou & Sjöblom, 1992), there has been particularly little research

Requests for reprints should be addressed to K. Niedl, Institute of Human Resource Management, University of Business Administration and Economics (Wirtschaftuniversität), Althanstrasse 51, 1090 Vienna, Austria.

[1] An earlier version of the paper was presented at the Seventh European Congress on Work and Organizational Psychology, 19–22 April 1995, Györ, Hungary.

on mobbing in the German-speaking countries. The topic has become a subject of interest only for the last four years. No empirical data can be found before 1994.

This article reports the results of two studies of mobbing carried out in Austria and Germany. After a short review of the literature, the relationship between mobbing and well-being will be investigated in a first study. The second study was an exploratory investigation of the organizational effects of mobbing in connection with coping behaviour.

Depending on the different instruments for the classification of persons as bullied/non-bullied and the socioeconomical conditions of the different organizations/countries in which the studies were carried out, the number of affected persons varies widely (Björkqvist et al., 1994; Einarsen & Raknes, 1991; Leymann, 1991a; Matthiesen et al., 1989; Papaioannou & Sjöblom, 1992; Skogstad et al., 1990; Thylefors, 1987; Vartia, 1991). In these different studies from 1% (Einarsen & Raknes, 1991) up to 21.6% (Leymann, 1992 in a study of disabled people) out of a specified population were classified as bullied employees. Similar results could be found in field studies with school children (Munthe, 1989; Smith & Thompson, 1991).

Most of the studies focused on the individual effects of mobbing. Brodsky (1976, p. 38) states that "the effect of harassment upon its victims can be devastating". In a Norwegian study 21.6% of the 2095 people who were surveyed, reported reduced well-being because of mobbing. They were especially affected by depression followed by other psychological and somatic impairments (Einarsen & Raknes, 1991). In a Finnish survey, bullied persons showed significantly more psychosomatic and depressive symptoms than non-bullied persons (Papaioannou & Sjöblom, 1992). In another Finnish study the bullied employees showed significantly higher depression, anxiety, aggression, and symptoms of post-traumatic stress disorders (Björkqvist et al., 1994). These findings support the results of various studies carried out by Leymann (1991b), Aggressive and auto-aggressive behaviour can also result as an extreme consequence of mobbing. Leymann (1990) supposed that 10–15% of the yearly suicides in Sweden can be explained by this kind of hostile background.

Only a small number of authors focus on the organizational effects of bullying as a consequence of reduced well-being. This point is important primarily because of the possibility of identifying mobbing actions in an early phase of the process. This perspective is also important for the motivation of an organization's management to support employee assistance or other prevention approaches. In a Norwegian study, 2.8% of a sample of 2141 reported that they had stayed away from their workplace because of mobbing (Einarsen & Raknes, 1991). The correlation between absenteeism and mobbing in a Norwegian study among nurses was weak and not significant, but the correlation between absenteeism and the perception that others were bullied at work was higher and significant (Matthiesen et al., 1989).

A Norwegian study among teachers also demonstrated weak correlations between absenteeism from work and mobbing (Matthiesen et al., 1989). In an Australian study, those employees who were confronted with mobbing reported significantly more short-term and long-term absenteeism (Toohey, 1991). Another organizational impact of mobbing can be seen in a higher readiness for leaving the organization. Out of a sample of 99 bullied employees in a Finnish study, 46% reported that they had thought about leaving their jobs (Vartia, 1991). In a Norwegian study among teachers the perception of mobbing or the fact that someone was bullied himself/herself showed high correlation with an intention to quit the job (Matthiesen et al., 1989). A Norwegian study also demonstrated that the respondents perceived a negative impact of mobbing in form of lost productivity: Out of a sample of 2083 respondents, 27% reported that mobbing at work reduces work effectiveness (Einarsen & Raknes, 1991). In summary, the findings show the tendency of higher absenteeism and turnover rates as well as a reduced level of productivity. However, the findings reveal a low consistency in their results. In addition, a discussion about the precise conditions for the occurrence of these consequences is needed.

METHOD

Research Questions

As previously mentioned, there has been relatively little research on mobbing in the German-speaking countries. Due to socioeconomic and cultural factors one should be careful when transferring data from one country to another. With this in mind, data from an Austrian organization were collected to compare with already existing results from Scandinavian studies. The first aim of this study is to investigate the prevalence of mobbing by applying a translated questionnaire that had already been used in Sweden. Secondly, a comparison of the bullied/non-bullied employees concerning the well-being of these two groups offers the opportunity to evaluate the individual effects of mobbing.

Although there has been a lot or research on the effects of well-being, there exists relatively little research on so-called "organizational effects". As previously shown, the current results regarding organizational effects of mobbing are frugal. Present studies normally focus on the amount and length of absenteeism or the level of productivity and neglect the fact that mobbing is a complex process as has been shown by few researchers (e.g. Björkqvist, 1992; Brodsky, 1976; Leymann, 1990). Considering this, the study aims at investigating the following question: In what way do employees cope with mobbing during the whole process starting from the time they first perceive mobbing? In order to explore the possible strategies of a bullied employee, an explorative study will be carried out.

Study I

To investigate the prevalence of mobbing in Austria and to assess the question of well-being, employees of a public hospital were examined. The participants of this study consisted of 368 employees of an Austrian public hospital. This sample included three different professional groups consisting of the medical group (e.g. physicians, psychologists), the nursing group (e.g. nurses, assistant nurses, school nurses), and the administration group (e.g. keyboard operators, maintenance workers). The main demographic characteristics are shown in Table 1.

To obtain data which are comparable with those from Sweden, a revised German version of the LIPT (Leymann Inventory of Psychological Terror) was used (Leymann, 1989). The questionnaire contains the following sections on: (1) background information including sex, age, profession, and position, (2) a catalogue of 45 hostile actions, (3) questions on number, position, and sex of the aggressors, and (4) a catalogue of stress symptoms. The questionnaire contains the question "Have you been subjected to one or more of the following actions during the last 12 months?" If the answer is "Yes", the respondent has to answer for how long and how often he/she has been subjected to a specific hostile action. The options for alternative frequencies are: daily/almost daily/once a week/several times a month/seldom/never; and for the duration: longer than five years/between two and five years/about one year/about half a year/longer than two months/shorter

TABLE 1
Main Demographical Characteristics of
the Respondents in the Public Hospital
Sample ($N = 368$)

	%
Sex	
female	61.4
male	38.6
Age	
20 or younger	2.2
21 to 30	29.6
31 to 40	39.3
41 to 50	23.5
51 or older	5.3
Nationality	
Austria	91.0
Germany	1.1
formerly Yugoslavia	4.8
others	3.1

than two months. Leymann's criterion for the classification of a person as "bullied/non-bullied" was used. According to this criterion, a person is bullied when he or she is affected by at least one or more of the 45 hostile actions listed in the LIPT-catalogue at least once a week and over a period of at least half a year.

Instead of the original LIPT-stress scale, the subjects rated their well-being in five different scales. The scales of "psychological impairment of well-being" by Mohr comprise scales of (1) depression, (2) self-esteem, (3) anxiety, (4) irritation, and (5) psychosomatic symptoms (Mohr, 1986). Psychometric properties of the scales and item examples are given in Table 2.

The study was carried out as a postal survey. The questionnaire was distributed to all 1264 employees of the hospital with the request to fill in the questionnaire and to return it to internal post-boxes. Two versions of the questionnaire were used: a German and a Serbo-Croatian version. The response rate in the public hospital was 29% ($N = 368$) which is satisfying considering the sensitivity of the topic.

Study II

To examine the organizational effects of mobbing, an in-patient group was investigated. Concerning the taboo of the topic of mobbing in Austria, it seems possible only up to a certain extent to receive "true" answers in respect to organizational effects. Therefore, a sample of German in-patients was surveyed. This sample consisted of 10 German in-patients who had experienced bullying in their workplace. The participants of this "in-patient group" showed different psychological and/or psychosomatic symptoms. They were all participants of a six-week rehabilitation programme at a German hospital and they all shared one common denominator: They had left their firm because of mobbing. The sample ($N = 10$) consisted of six

TABLE 2
Scales by Mohr (1986); Examples for Items

Scale Item	Example
Depression	I feel lonesome, even when together with other people
Irritation	being irritated nervous
Psychosomatic complaints	headache backpain sleep disturbances
Self-esteem	I am OK I am proud of my achievements
Anxiety	I avoid contact with my superior

men and four women. The mean age was 42.5 years. Seven people were married; four participants came from the private and six participants from the public sector.

Open-ended problem focused interviews were conducted with the in-patients in order to collect data for the mobbing process. These interviews were theoretically based on the EVLN-model by Withey and Cooper (1989), which suggests four "final" reactions when people are unhappy at work. These final reactions can be either *exit*, *voice*, *loyalty*, or *neglect* (hence EVLN): People who are dissatisfied at work can focus attention on nonwork interests (reduction of commitment, neglect); people can improve their situation through voice (active problem solving); another possibility is to stay and support the organization with loyalty (passive hope of problem solving); people who are unhappy at work can also quit their job (exit). According to this model, dissatisfied employees choose those acts which are efficacious and whose costs are low for the individual, and also choose the setting which is attractive for the individual. Based on the EVLN-model, costs, efficacy, and the setting were translated into more specific terms (e.g. What alternatives for another job do you have? What factors prevent you from leaving the firm?). The in-patients were requested to reconstruct their process from that point onwards they had perceived mobbing for the first time. The interviews were recorded and then transcribed. The resulting qualitative data were then structured according to the EVLN-model.

RESULTS

Study I

Leymann (1993) suggested an operational definition of mobbing. A person is affected by mobbing if at least one of the 45 mobbing actions listed in the LIPT questionnaire occurred at least once a week and for at least six months. According to this criterion, a minimum of 7.8% (98 persons) or a maximum of 26.6% in the hospital can be classified as bullied. The minimum per-centage is calculated by the ratio "bullied persons/all employees" and the maximum by the ratio "bullied persons/sample". Two comparable studies carried out in Sweden show a lower percentage: The percentage in a sawmill was 1.7% and in a steel-mill 2.7% (Leymann, 1993; Leymann & Tallgren, 1987). Compared to a Swedish representative study in which a percentage of 3.5% was reported by Leymann (1991a), there is a tendency of a higher affectiveness in this Austrian organization although the data should not be considered as representative of all salaried employees.

The employees of the public hospital rated their well-being on the five scales of Mohr (1986). Table 3 shows the differences with regard to well-being of bullied/non-bullied employees in this organization. With the excep-

TABLE 3
Scores of Mohr-Scales of Bullied and Non-bullied Employees in the Public Hospital

	Bullied			Non-bullied			
	N	Mean	SD	N	Mean	SD	t
Irritation	95	3.74	1.17	266	3.20	1.12	3.88**
Depression	96	2.90	1.33	264	2.38	1.03	3.49**
Psychosomatic complaints	96	2.45	0.93	267	2.01	0.74	4.18**
Anxiety	95	2.53	1.34	265	2.08	0.93	3.06**
Self-esteem	97	1.86	0.86	267	1.79	0.64	0.73^{ns}

$**P < 0.01$; ^{ns} = not significant.

tion of the scale "self-esteem" all means were highly significant among bullied/non-bullied persons whereas there were some differences in respect to the gender of the bullied employees.

The differences regarding well-being in respect to sex can be seen in Table 4. No effects occurred for irritation, depression, and self-esteem. Bullied women reported a significantly higher mean of psychosomatic complaints as well as a higher level of anxiety.

In summary, the present results confirm the findings from other comparable studies that mobbing has a negative impact on the well-being of an individual. Given that women tend to report higher levels of psychological complaints in general, there is no clear evidence that women's health is more affected by mobbing than the health of men.

TABLE 4
Scores of Mohr-Scales of Bullied Men and Women in the Public Hospital

	Bullied Men			Bullied Women			
	N	Mean	SD	N	Mean	SD	t
Irritation	35	3.55	0.79	60	3.85	1.34	1.38^{ns}
Depression	35	2.59	1.06	61	3.09	1.43	1.95^{ns}
Psychosomatic complaints	35	2.14	0.74	61	2.62	0.99	2.74**
Anxiety	34	2.15	0.93	61	2.74	1.49	2.38*
Self-esteem	35	1.81	0.63	62	1.90	0.97	0.55^{ns}

$*P < 0.05$; $**P < 0.01$; ^{ns} = not significant.

Study II

The aim of the second study was to explore possible individual strategies related to mobbing which had an impact on the organization. As mentioned previously the qualitative data were structured by the EVLN-model used to analyse the process of mobbing with regard to the organizational effects. The qualitative data were classified in process phases asking the question: Which of the four possible reactions to mobbing did the person show over a period of time? The results are shown in Fig. 1. The position of the first number in each line illustrates the first reaction of the employee when he or she realizes that he or she is affected by mobbing (e.g. person 1 first

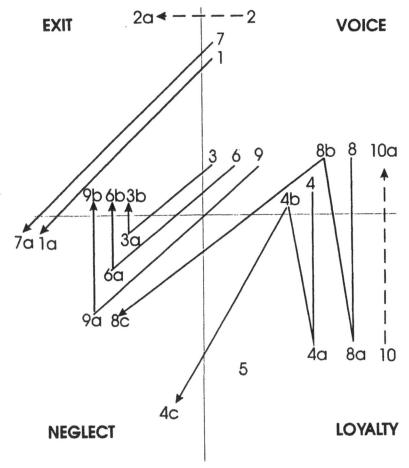

FIG. 1. Coping-behaviour related to mobbing, structured by the EVLN-model for the "in-patient-group" ($N = 10$).

attempts active problem solving—voice). The following numbers illustrate the second reaction in the process when the first one is not satisfying (e.g. person 1 then reacts by neglecting his/her work—neglect, 1a).

Mobbing perceived by person 8 lasted for 2.5 years. The first coping behaviour of person 8 can be understood as constructive problem solving (voice, 8). He tried to inform his superior who, however, did not react. After the situation had not improved he thought that the best strategy would be waiting (loyalty, 8a). The situation deteriorated more and more and the employee aimed again at an improvement of the situation by discussing the problem with his superior (voice, 8b). The employee showed different psychosomatic complaints which were confirmed by a physician. Finally, he reacted with a reduction of commitment (neglect, 8c). As can be seen from the figure, most of the patients first reacted with constructive coping (voice, loyalty) to their problematic situation. After perceiving that problem solving was not possible, the reactions turned to "destructive" forms such as leaving the firm (exit) or reducing commitment (neglect). Most of the "final reactions" were of this type.

The explorative results indicate that the individuals surveyed did not cope using simple "fight or flight" strategies but showed a more complex sequence of reactions influenced by different factors. Therefore, the process of mobbing must be taken into account when organizational effects are regarded.

DISCUSSION

To summarize the main findings, we observed a tendency for the employees of an Austrian hospital to perceive more bullying compared to the Swedish results. However, limitations considering comparability (e.g. cultural, socioeconomic aspects) and the instrument LIPT must be taken into account. The results indicate that mobbing is not restricted to single cases. A marked segment of employees perceive hostile treatment by peers, subordinates, or executives.

Bullied persons showed a negative impact on well-being (anxiety, depression, irritation, psychosomatic complaints) in comparison with non-bullied persons. These results indicate that personnel development managers have to make provision for impaired employees, in practice by employing, internally or externally, employee assistance professionals.

At the end of the process, the people who were bullied showed destructive reactions in respect to organizational effects. Although there were individual differences, most of the final reactions included two destructive types: reducing commitment (neglect) or leaving the firm (exit). This implies a need for training managers to monitor the early indicators of conflict to prevent a deterioration of the mobbing coping behaviour as described previously.

Normally, organizational effects are expressed in terms of cost. A precise calculation of the costs of mobbing is not possible because of the singularity of the individual conditions, actions, and duration. However, a series of studies show that relationship between reduced well-being and negative organizational effects such as reduced turnover, higher absenteeism, and lower productivity (e.g. Howell & Crown, 1971; Jenkins, 1980; Shepherd & Barraclough, 1980; Toohey, 1991). With regard to these results, mobbing should be seen as a cost factor influencing work effectiveness. Therefore, in an organizational context, it is the responsibility of personnel development managers to set up systems for preventing mobbing.

REFERENCES

Björkqvist, K. (1992). Trakassering förekommer bland anställda vid ÅA. *Meddelanden från Åbo Akademi, 9,* 14–17.

Björkqvist, K., Österman, K., & Hjelt-Bäck, M. (1994). Aggression among university employees. *Aggressive Behavior, 20,* 173–184.

Bolger, N., DeLongis, A., Kessler, R., & Schilling, E. (1989). Effects of daily stress on negative mood. *Journal of Personality and Social Psychology, 57,* 808–818.

Brodsky, C. (1976). *The harassed worker.* Toronto: Lexington Books, DC Heath & Company.

Einarsen, S., & Raknes, B.I. (1991). *Mobbing i arbeidslivet. En undersøkelse av forekomst og helsemessige konsekvenser av mobbing på norske arbeidplasser.* Bergen: Forskningssenter for Arbeidsmiljø, Helse og Sikkerhet (FAHS), Universitetet i Bergen.

Howell, R., & Crown, S. (1971). Sickness absence levels and personality inventory scores. *British Journal of Industrial Medicine, 28,* 126–130.

Jenkins, R. (1980). Minor psychiatric morbidity and its contribution to sickness absence. *British Journal of Industrial Medicine, 42,* 147–154.

Kahn, R.L. (1973). Conflict, ambiguity, and overload: Three elements in job stress. *Occupational Mental Health, 3,* 2–9.

Leymann, H. (1989). *Presentation av LIPT-formuläret: konstruktion, validering, utfall.* Stockholm: Praktikertjänst AB.

Leymann, H. (1990). Mobbing and psychological terror at workplaces. *Violence and Victims, 5,* 119–126.

Leymann, H. (1991a). *Vuxenmobbning på svenska arbetsplatser. En rikstäckande undersökning med 2438 intervjuer.* Delrapport 1. Stockholm: Arbetarskyddsstyrelsen.

Leymann, H. (1991b). *Psykiatriska problem vid vuxenmobbning. En rikstäckande undersökning med 2438 intervjuer.* Delrapport 3. Stockholm: Arbetarskyddsstyrelsen.

Leymann, H. (1992). *Lönebidrag och mobbad. En svag grupps psykosociala arbetsvillkor i Sverige.* Stockholm: Arbetarskyddsstyrelsen.

Leymann, H. (1993). *Mobbing—Psychoterror am Arbeitsplatz und wie man sich dagegen wehren kann [Mobbing—psychoterror at work and how one can defend oneself].* Reinbeck: Rowohlt.

Leymann, H., & Gustavsson, B. (1984). *Psykiskt våld i arbetslivet. Två explorativa undersökningar [Psychological violence at workplaces. Two explorative studies].* Undersökningsrapport 42. Stockholm: Arbetarskyddsstyrelsen.

Leymann, H., & Tallgren, U. (1987). *Investigation into the frequency of adult mobbing in a Swedish steel company using the LIPT questionnaire.* Unpublished paper. Stockholm.

Matthiesen, S.B., Raknes, B.I., & Rökkum, O. (1989). Mobbing på arbeidsplassen [Bullying at work]. *Tidsskrift for Norsk Psykologforening, 26,* 761–774.

Mergner, U. (1989). Zur sozialen Konstitution psychischer Belastung durch Arbeit. Konzeptionelle Überlegungen und empirische Konkretionen [On the social constitution of psychological stress: Conceptual considerations and empirical implications]. *Zeitschrift für Arbeits- und Organisationpsychologie, 33,* 64–72.

Mohr, G. (1986). *Die Erfassung psychischer Befindensbeeinträchtigungen bei Industriearbeitern. [The measurement of psychological dysfunctioning of workers].* Frankfurt a.M.: Peter Lang.

Munthe, E. (1989). Bullying in Scandinavia. In E. Munthe (Ed.), *Bullying: An international perspective* (pp. 66–90). London: David Fulton Publishers.

Paanen, T., & Vartia, M. (1991). *Henkinen väkivalta työpaikoilla. Kysely- ja haastattelututkimus valtion työterveyshuollossa ja työterveyshuollon auttamiskeinot [Mobbing at workplaces in state government].* Helsinki: Työterveyslaitos, psykologian osasto.

Papaioannou, S., & Sjöblom, L. (1992). *Arbetsplatstrakassering i kvinnodominerad vårdmiljö.* Åbo: Åbo Akademi, humanistiska fakulteten, psykologiska institutionen.

Shepherd, D., & Barraclough, B. (1980). Work and suicide: An empirical investigation. *British Journal of Psychiatry, 136,* 469–478.

Skogstad, A., Matthiesen, S., & Hellesøy, O. (1990). *Hjelpepleiernes Arbeidsmiljøkvalitet. En undersøkelse av arbeidsmiljø, helse og trivsel blant hjelpepleierne i Hordaland.* Bergen: Forskningssenter for Arbeidsmiljø, Helse og Sikkerhet (FAHS), Universitetet Bergen.

Smith, P., & Thompson, D. (1991). Dealing with bully/victim problems in the U.K. In E. Munthe (Ed.), *Bullying: An international perspective* (pp. 1–12). London: David Fulton Publishers.

Thylefors, I. (1987). *Syndabockar. Om utstötning och mobbning i arbetslivet [Scapegoats. On exclusions and bullying in working life].* Stockholm: Natur och Kultur.

Toohey, J. (1991). *Occupational stress: Managing a metaphor.* Unpublished dissertation. Graduate School of Management, Macquarie University, Sydney.

Vartia, M. (1991). Bullying at workplaces. In S. Lehtinene, J. Rantanen, P. Juuti, A. Koskela, K. Lindström, P. Rehnström, & J. Saari (Eds.), *Towards the 21st century: Work in the 1990s: Proceedings from the International Symposium on Future Trends in the Changing Working Life* (pp. 131–135). Helsinki: Institute of Occupational Health.

Withey, M., & Cooper, W. (1989). Predicting exit, voice, loyalty, and neglect. *Administrative Science Quarterly, 34,* 521–539.

Zapf, D., & Frese, M. (1991). Soziale Stressoren am Arbeitsplatz und psychische Gesundheit [Social stressors at work and psychological health]. In S. Greif, E. Bamberg, & N.K. Semmer (Eds.), Psychischer Streß am Arbeitsplatz (pp. 168–184). Göttingen: Hogrefe.

EUROPEAN JOURNAL OF WORK AND ORGANIZATIONAL PSYCHOLOGY, 1996, 5 (2), 251–275

Mobbing at Work and the Development of Post-traumatic Stress Disorders

Heinz Leymann and Annelie Gustafsson

University of Umeå, Sweden

Psychosocial research on mobbing is currently being carried out in a number of countries, mainly in Europe. Mobbing is defined as an extreme social stressor at workplaces. In this article, its serious mental and psychosomatic health consequences are demonstrated and discussed. A factor analysis of symptom statistics collected through answers from a study representative of the entire Swedish workforce showed post-traumatic stress disorder (PTSD) as the plausible diagnosis. In addition, 64 patients subjected to mobbing at their work places are diagnosed with the co-operation of a rehabilitation clinic specializing in the treatment of chronic PTSD. The statistical analysis of these 64 diagnoses shows a severe degree of PTSD, with mental effects fully comparable with PTSD from war or prison camp experiences.

INTRODUCTION—EARLIER RESEARCH

In the autumn of 1993, the Swedish National Board of Occupational Safety and Health stipulated a ruling of legal character which forbids psychosocial victimization (mobbing) at the workplace (AFS, 1993). Mobbing and expulsion from the labour market would thereby, if not totally prevented, at least be limited. This ruling was the result of research carried out during the 10 years before its legislation: This most problematic and dangerous health-damaging factor at workplaces, the phenomenon of mobbing, was first described by Leymann and Gustavsson in 1984. Numerous studies have since been financed by the Swedish Work Environment Fund (Leymann, 1986, 1988, 1990, 1992a, 1992b, 1992c, 1992d). During the early 1990s, a number of research programmes began in different countries: Austria (Niedl, 1995), Norway (Einarsen & Raknes, 1991), Finland (Paanen & Vartia, 1991), and Germany (Becker, 1993; Zapf, Knorz, & Kulla, this issue). Journalistic and clinical observations have also been reported in the USA, England (Adams, 1992), Australia, and Denmark. All these reports have in common the very severe health consequences of mobbing at work.

Requests for reprints should be addressed to H. Leymann, Bastionsgatan 23, S-371 32 Karlskrona, Sweden.

The clinical breakthrough came in the beginning of the 1990s when Leymann (1992d) discovered that post-traumatic stress disorder (PTSD) is probably the correct psychiatric and psychological diagnosis for approximately 95% of the subjected individuals.

In the present article we will first describe the mobbing concept and PTSD-symptoms. In a second step we will present some factor analytical results of a Swedish representative study on mobbing which shows that the symptoms of ill-health found in mobbing victims fit the description of PTSD. Next we will present results of the analysis of 64 patients from a clinic for the treatment of mobbing victims. Finally, we will summarize the most important findings and draw some conclusions.

THE MOBBING PHENOMENON

Mobbing has been referred to as "ganging up on someone", "bullying", or "psychological terror". In this type of conflict, the victim is subjected to a systematic stigmatization process and encroachment of his or her civil rights. After a few years, it may ultimately lead to the expulsion from the labour market if the individual in question is unable to find employment.

Mobbing at work involves hostile and unethical communication towards an individual, who is pushed into a helpless and defenceless position. According to definition this must occur very frequently (statistical definition: at least once a week) and over a long period of time (statistical definition: at least six months). Because of the high frequency and long duration of hostile behaviour, this maltreatment results in considerable psychological, psychosomatic, and social suffering. Research so far reveals a number of typical phases. A description of the phenomenon can be found in Leymann (this issue).

The Discovery of PTSD as a Diagnosis Following Victimization at Work

In connection with the Work Environment Fund's (AMFO) large investment in a research project concerning social expulsion, mobbing, and victimization at work in the labour market, an interview series employing the LIPT-method (Leymann, 1990) was included in one of the national representative investigations (Leymann, 1992a). This sample included 2428 subjects. Analyses revealed that 350 of these had been subjected to mobbing. The individuals replied to questions regarding a number of stress symptoms chosen from neurological questionnaires in use at the Department of Neurology at the Swedish National Board of Occupational Health Research Institute. For each symptom, the interviewed individual had to state whether he or she had had the symptom during the last 12 months

(1) very often or constantly, (2) often, (3) less often or seldom, or (4) never (complete information about sample and methods can be found in the original report from Leymann, 1992a). The further statistical analysis of the material led to the hypothesis that a PTSD (post-traumatic stress disorder) and GAD (general anxiety disorder) would be appropriate psychiatric diagnoses. The results of the statistical analysis and symptoms of PTSD as defined will be presented first; then PTSD will be explained.

Results from the Factor Analysis

The statistical processing included of a factor analysis of symptoms (Leymann, 1992d). The principle component varimax rotation was used. As a basis for the analysis the results of all responses from identified mobbing victims were used. The symptoms occurring over the past 12 months led to formation of seven factor groups (see Table 1). All 350 of the identified mobbing victims were interviewed.

The first five factor groups show the most revealing factor profiles. From a clinical perspective, these five groups are neither medically nor psychiatrically difficult to interpret. Group 1 deals with cognitive effects of strong

TABLE 1
Factor Analysis and Item Weights of Symptoms Stated by Employees
Reporting Mobbing Activities (*N* = 350)

Group 1		*Group 3*	
Memory disturbances	0.5	Chest pain	0.6
Concentration difficulties	0.5	Sweating	0.6
Low-spirited, depressed	0.5	Dryness of the mouth	0.5
Lack of initiative, apathetic	0.6	Heart palpitations	0.6
Easily irritated	0.7	Shortness of breath	0.7
General restlessness	0.7	Blood surgings	0.8
Aggressive	0.6	*Group 4*	
Feeling of insecurity	0.6	Backache	0.7
Sensitive to setbacks	0.8	Neck pain (posterior)	0.7
		Muscular pain	0.6
Group 2		*Group 5*	
Nightmares	0.6	Difficulties falling asleep	0.6
Abdominal or stomach pain	0.6	Interrupted sleep	0.7
Diarrhoea	0.7	Early awakening	0.7
Vomiting	0.7	*Group 6*	
Feeling of sickness	0.8	Weakness in legs	0.6
Loss of appetite	0.6	Feebleness	0.6
Lump in throat	0.5	*Group 7*	
Crying	0.5	Fainting	0.8
Lonely, contactless	0.6	Tremor	0.6

stressors producing psychological hyper-reactions. Group 2 indicates a syndrome with psychosomatic stress symptoms. Group 3 deals with symptoms arising in connection with production of stress hormones and activities of the autonomic nervous system. Group 4 describes symptoms which company health-care physicians often encounter in individuals who have been stressed for very long periods of time and where the symptoms deal with muscular tension. Group 5 comprises symptoms concerning sleep problems.

These results were compared with well-known psychiatric syndromes as described in the manuals of psychiatric diagnoses (*DSM-III-R*, American Psychiatric Association, 1987; *ICD-10*, World Health Organization, 1992) leading to the hypothesis that PTSD may be the fitting diagnosis. These symptom groups generated (groups 1 to 5 in Table 1) fall psychiatrically under the *DSM-III-R* category "anxiety disorders". The groupings or parts of these are described under the diagnosis "post-traumatic stress disorder" (PTSD), but also under "generalized anxiety disorder" (GAD).

Examining the diagnostic criteria for "generalized anxiety disorder", we find the factor groups 4, 6, and 7 amongst the DSM group "motor tension", factor groups 2 and 3 in the DSM group "autonomic hyperactivity", and factor groups 1 and 5 in the DSM group "vigilance and scanning". The diagnostic criteria for "post-traumatic stress disorder" corresponds with factor groups 1 and 5.

What then is a post-traumatic stress disorder?

What is PTSD?

As mentioned previously, two authoritative psychiatric diagnosis manuals exist. One, which will be presented here, is edited by the American Psychiatric Association. The other (*ICD-10*) is published by the World Health Organization (1992) in Geneva. The guidelines for post-traumatic stress disorder, according to the American *DSM-III-R*, are divided into five criteria groups.

A. The individual has witnessed something beyond usual human experiences and which would be very trying for almost anybody, e.g. a serious threat against one's life, one's physical, or one's psychological integrity; a serious threat against or injury of one's children, partner, or even other close relatives or friends; sudden and extensive destruction of one's home or home district; seeing a person who has just been seriously injured or killed due to an accident or violent act, or witnessing the entire course of events.

B. The traumatic event is relived repeatedly in *at least one* of the following ways: (1) Returning, insistent, and painful memory images of the events; (2) Recurring nightmares about the event; (3) The individual can suddenly act or feel as if the traumatic event is repeated (included is a feeling of going through the event again, illusions, hallucinations, and dissociative episodes or flashbacks, even such that occur during awakening or under the influence of drugs); (4) Intensive psychological discomfort in the presence of events that symbolize or are similar to some aspect of the traumatic event, e.g. the anniversary of the trauma.

C. The individual constantly avoids stimuli that can be associated with the trauma or shows a general blunting of ability to react emotionally (which was not present before the trauma) in *at least three*, of the following: (1) Efforts to avoid thoughts or feelings that are associated with the trauma; (2) Efforts to avoid activities or situations that arouse memories of the trauma; (3) Inability to remember some important aspect of the trauma (psychogenic amnesia); (4) Marked reduced interest in important activities; (5) Feeling of a lack of interest or expulsion by others; (6) Limited affects, e.g. inability to cherish loving feelings; (7) A feeling of not having any future, not expecting to have a career, get married, have children, or live a long life.

D. Permanent signs of hypersensitivity (which were not present before the trauma) are shown in *at least two* of the following: (1) Difficulties in falling asleep or uneasy sleep; (2) Irritability or bursts of fury; (3) Concentration difficulties; (4) Tense vigilance; (5) Exaggerated reaction to unexpected external stimuli; (6) Physiological reactions in the presence of events that symbolize or are similar to some aspects of the traumatic event.

E. The disturbance must be present for *at least one month* (with symptoms according to groups B, C, and D).

As reported previously, the factor analysis carried out also revealed a connection with the *DSM-III-R* psychiatric diagnosis "general anxiety disorder" (GAD). The interesting criteria group in the GAD diagnosis is its group D.

General Anxiety Disorder

Patient PTSD values were so high (the majority received "full scores"), that we used the GAD criteria group D as a "magnifying glass" for the PTSD criteria group D. The reason is partly the desire to acquire differential diagnoses between the patients and partly to verify the clinical observation that the symptoms in PTSD criteria group D often worsen (more symptoms, deeper penetration) during prolonged and deepened PTSD reactions.

The GAD criteria group D allows differentiation of psychosomatic stress symptoms into three groups concerning somatic tensions (*muscular tension*), consequential symptoms of hormonal activity (*autonomic nervous system hyperactivity*), and symptoms which point out cognitive mental activities or malfunctions (*tense vigilance and hypersensitivity*). At least six of the following 18 symptoms should be present in connection with anxiety feelings (does not include symptoms that are *only* present in connection with panic attacks):

Regarding muscular tension: (1) Trembling, jumpy, shaky. (2) Tense, aching or sore muscles. (3) Restlessness. (4) Unusual tiredness.

Regarding autonomic nervous system hyperactivity: (5) Air hunger or a feeling of shortness of breath. (6) Heart palpitations or rapid pulse. (7) Sweating or cold wet hands. (8) Dryness of the mouth. (9) Dizziness or giddiness. (10) Feeling of sickness, diarrhoea, or other gastro-intestinal difficulties. (11) Feeling of suddenly being quite warm or cold. (12) Frequent need to urinate. (13) Difficulties in swallowing or "lump in the throat".

Regarding tense vigilance and hypersensitivity: (14) Affected or "up-tight". (15) Over-reacting to unexpected external stimuli. (16) Concentration difficulties or "completely blank mind". (17) Difficulties in falling asleep or uneasy sleep.

Another diagnostically very important notion derived from the manuals on psychiatric diagnoses concerns whether the subjected individual's personality essentially affects diagnostic outcome.

Personality as a Diagnostic Feature

One quite often hears the theory that a harassed person's "premorbid personality" should be blamed as the social trigger for mobbing situations. This notion is also widespread amongst professionals. But until today, empirical research on adult mobbing, which began in 1982, has not been able to relate the cause of a mobbing process to the victim's personality. Not even similar research concerning child mobbing in schools (e.g. Olweus, 1993) has shown such a connection.

The *ICD-10* and the *DSM-II-R* state that PTSD in its chronic phase can result in a permanent personality change. The WHO manual *ICD-10* (1992) describes typical symptoms found in individuals suffering from chronic PTSD. This change, according to our clinical observations, seems to predominate in one of two anxiety effects (in rare cases in both), either a serious depression or a serious obsession. We have individuals with both symptoms, mainly being individuals who, after several years of trying to protect themselves, still are suffering from lengthy and daily victimization at work.

In our clinical work we have, therefore, modified and broadened the *ICD-10* symptom descriptions. In the following list of symptoms, we have marked * the symptoms originally found in the *ICD-10*. Since obsession as the main characteristic is always accompanied by a certain depressiveness and vice versa, the following symptoms of the permanent personality change may be found in many patients.

Permanent personality change with mainly obsession predominating.
  1. A hostile and suspicious attitude towards the surroundings.*
  2. A chronic feeling of nervousness that one is in constant danger.*
  3. A compulsory accounting of one's own fate (which triggered PTSD) to a degree that exceeds the surrounding's limit of tolerance and which leads to isolation and loneliness.
  4. Hypersensitivity with respect to injustices and a constant identification with the suffering of others in a pathological, compulsory manner.

Permanent personality change with mainly depression as a predominate.
  5. A feeling of emptiness and hopelessness.*
  6. A chronic inability to experience joy from common events in everyday life.
  7. A constant risk of eventual psychopharmaca abuse.

Permanent personality change with additional symptoms that indicate that the patient has resigned.
  8. The individual isolates him- or herself.*
  9. The person no longer feels part of the society (alienating effect).*
  10. The person shows a cynical attitude towards the world around him or her.

Obviously, it is no longer possible to evaluate the victim's original personality during a chronic PTSD phase. What is diagnosed is the destruction of the personality. Since PTSD-injured individuals show the same syndrome and thereby the same behaviour and symptom mix (namely the syndrome that is called PTSD), it is common that professionals who are not experienced in the diagnosis of PTSD falsely assume that it is a certain type of personality that is affected by difficulties following violent events, mobbing, being taken hostage, rape, catastrophe, etc. (Leymann, 1989, 1995).

64 PATIENTS AT THE SWEDISH
REHABCENTER INC., VIOLEN

Both clinical experience as well as the statistical results reviewed in the previous section lead to the conclusion that individuals who have been subjected to intensive mobbing at their workplaces are at risk of developing post-traumatic stress disorders. In order to analyse the development of PTSD in more detail, we conducted a study for the first 64 patients at the Swedish RehabCenter Inc., Violen. This institution is a private clinic with a specially designed treatment programme for mobbing victims in a chronic PTSD phase.

Method and Procedure

In order to answer questions of more detailed aspects of PTSD, we carried out statistical analyses using the data collected in our diagnostic work at the clinic.

The majority of the patients were referred by the social insurance offices from different areas in the country. A small number were directly referred by the employer. According to the constitution of the Swedish National Board of Occupational Safety and Health (AFS, 1994), which has legal character, it is the employer's obligation to provide vocational rehabilitation for their employees when so required. All patients voluntarily came to the clinic.

Sweden's RehabCenter Inc., Violen specializes in the treatment of psychological effects that have arisen in connection with individuals being subjected to psychological trauma (e.g. bank robberies, industrial accidents, catastrophes, serious car accidents, victimization at work, etc.). The clinic offered a four-week indoor treatment programme.

Selection of Diagnostical Instruments and Summary of Their Scientific Backgrounds

A number of internationally well-documented catastrophic psychiatrical diagnostical instruments were used.

1. *Brief Psychiatric Rating Scale (BPRS by Overall & Gorham—an expert observation rating scale)*. Overall and Beller published two articles in 1984: "The brief psychiatric rating scale (BPRS) in geropsychiatric research: I. Factor structure on an inpatient unit" (Overall & Beller, 1984) and "The brief psychiatric rating scale (BPRS) in geropsychiatric research: II. Representative profile patterns" (Beller & Overall, 1984).

2. *Sleep and Alertness (The Caroline Institute Sleep Laboratory)*. The questionnaire we used is a shortened version of that used at the Caroline Institute Sleep Laboratory. Although the clinical experience behind the questionnaire is extensive, no metrical or statistical studies exist regarding the questionnaire's validity or reliability.

3. *General Health Questionnaire (GHQ by Goldberg, 20-version)*, The questionnaire's original version comprises 60 questions. For our diagnoses, a shortened version with 20 questions was used. The validations that were carried out by Norwegian researchers are by Malt (1989), "The validity of the general health questionnaire in a sample of accidentally injured adults" and by Holen (1990), "A long-term outcome study of survivors from a disaster". The original study was carried out by Goldberg (1985), "Identifying psychiatric illness among general medical patients" and by Goldberg and Williams (1988), "A user's guide to the general health questionnaire".

4. *Beck's Depression Inventory (BDI by Beck, 13-version)*. The questionnaire exists in different versions. The original version has 21 questions, the version used in our diagnoses is a shortened version with 13 questions. The first publication was released in 1961 by Beck, Ward, Mendelsohn, Mock, and Erbaugh.

5. *Impact of Event Scale (IES by Horowitz et al., 15 version)*. The questionnaire scale is a deepening of the criteria which are included in the conditions for diagnosis in the psychiatric diagnostic manual *DSM-III-R* (American Psychiatric Association, 1987), upon which this scale has been based. The scale was evaluated by Zilberg, Weiss, and Horowitz (1982), at the Langley Porter Psychiatric Institute at the University of California, San Francisco. The scale was originally published by Horowitz, Wilner, and Alvarez (1982a), "Impact of event scale: A measure of subjective distress".

6. *Post-traumatic Symptom Scale (PTSS-10 by Malt)*. The scale is described in Raphael, Lundin, and Weisaeth (1989), "A research method for the study of psychological and psychiatric aspects of disaster".

7. Middlesex Hospital Questionnaire (40-version). A large number of scientific articles about this questionnaire have appeared. A survey of the research is found in Sidney (1974), "The Middlesex Hospital questionnaire (MHQ) in clinical research: A review". A more recent article is found in Pallecchi, Nicolau, Biagi, and Nardini (1990), "The Middlesex Hospital questionnaire (MHQ) compared with the MMPI: Study of internal and reciprocal correlations between the psychodiagnostic scales".

8. *PTSD original diagnosis according to DSM-III-R*. This criteria list is taken directly from *DSM-III-R* (American Psychiatric Association, 1987) and was used as a diagnostic summary of the seven questionnaires mentioned in this list.

The Diagnosis Method

Following an occupational-social anamnesis, the diagnosis procedure was carried out. This included a chronological description of the traumatic course of events which had taken place during the past years. The anamnesis served as the basis for the diagnosis criteria part A, provided that the diagnosis showed a PTSD injury. These anamneses were carried out during interviews lasting approximately four to 10 hours.

The patients were informed that the diagnosis is done with help of standardized questionnaires. During the course of the interviews, as soon as the respective questionnaire was completed, the patient was notified about what type of information had been collected. Furthermore, patients were immediately informed about the results of his or her responses. Thus, the questionnaire was evaluated immediately and continuously throughout the ongoing interview. Even the diagnostic interpretations of the patients' answers were explained. If, for example, an individual answered "yes" to the questions concerning a decline in sexual interests, difficulties in making decisions, difficulties in starting everyday duties, etc., this initiated an explanation for the meaning of his or her depressiveness. The patient was thus not left with unanswered questions about what his or her answers *really* meant for his or her emotional state.

This method of diagnosing and simultaneously informing the patient thoroughly about the character and meaning of his or her answers may actually be regarded as a first cognitive behavioural therapeutic contribution already at this early stage during the contact with the patient. The diagnosis takes approximately two to four hours to complete. Patients are also told what the different criteria groups of the PTSD diagnosis mean and how they give rise to the psychosomatic symptoms in the diagnosis criteria group D.

The 64 Patient Diagnoses

What kinds of patients were seen at the clinic? What occupational branches did they come from? In what mental and physical conditions did they arrive? This will be discussed under two sections below regarding the patients bio- and socio-economical as well as their diagnostical data.

The Patients' Bio- and Socio-economical Data

The Number of Patients and Gender Information

64 patients were seen; 20 (31%) were men and 44 (69%) women. The gender distribution cannot be interpreted in respect to conditions on a national scale, and indicates only the percentual distribution between men and women among the patients who happened to be referred to us.

Age

The majority of the patients were between 41 and 50 years old (53% or 34 individuals); 23% or 15 individuals were between 51 and 60 years of age; 13% or 8 individuals were between 31 and 40 years; 5% or 3 individuals were either over 61 years old or under 30 respectively. For one individual, age information is missing. A correlation between age and gender indicates that women and men had the same age distribution.

Position

14 individuals (22%) had work leadership assignments, the others did not.

Occupation

Table 2 shows patient affiliation in 11 occupational groups. These con- stitute a summary of Sweden's statistical year book's (*Svenska statens statistika årsbok*, 1994) trade survey (see its Table 204: Gainfully employed

TABLE 2
The Patients' Trade Affiliation in Comparison with the Gainfully Employed Population's
Trade Affiliation in Sweden—The Patient Group (N = 64) is Not Representative

Trade	The Patient Groups at the Clinic (%)	Sweden's Working Population (%)	Over (+) or Under (−) Representation
01 Industrial companies	6.3	19.7	−
02 Trade, stockroom work	1.6	11.6	−
03 Public administration and social work (child, elderly care, etc.)	23.4	12.5	+
04 Forest/farming	3.1	2.7	
05 Health care	23.4	10.3	+
06 School/university	6.3	6.2	
07 Religious organizations	6.3	0.6	+
08 Administration and office	7.8 ⎫	11.8	
09 Technical/data	7.8 ⎭		
10 Bank and auditing	4.7	3.6	
11 Other	9.4	21.0	−

population according to branch of business or industry in November 1991
with exception for lines 8 and 9). The centre column of Table 2 gives the
expected percentage according to the country's population.

It must be pointed out that public administration and social work (which
includes child and elderly care), health care, and work in religious organizations (which includes the Swedish church) are over-represented, whereas
industrial companies (manufacturing and mechanical industry), trade and
stockroom work, together with other branches of business or industry are
under-represented. Our patient group was thus not nationally representative for all employees diagnosed with PTSD due to victimization at work or
other reasons. Other studies show, nevertheless, corresponding trends
(Leymann, 1992a, 1992b, 1992c, 1992e; Leymann & Gustafsson, in press;
Leymann & Lindroth, 1993; Leymann & Tallgren, 1989).

Diagnosis

In 59 individuals PTSD was diagnosed, the remaining five suffered from
dystymi (popularly expressed as psychological burnout). These five had the
same scores in the PTSD categories B to E, but lacked a traumatic course
of events in their occupational situation.

The Patients' Average Strain Period

By strain time we mean the length of time during which the patients
were subjected to mobbing activities resulting in emotional strain. The strain
time which the patients had to experience was very long. This period was

estimated from the time at which the patient's psychosocial working environment had become mentally disturbing until it became traumatic (for a chronological description of the phases in the process, see Leymann, 1992b, this issue).

In Table 3, it can be seen that only 15% of the patients has a strain period of less than one year. Just as many, namely 15%, had a strain period exceeding eight years! Most of the patients, 54%, had a strain period of between two and eight years. There was no difference between women and men.

Results from Diagnostical Instruments

In this section results are presented regarding the various diagnostical instruments used at the clinic. This will be done in four subsections, starting with instruments allowing detailed analyses of the PTSD-state. Thereafter results from two instruments are presented, including comprehensive data. In a third subsection we find results from differential diagnostics and finally data on the remaining quality of life.

Three Instruments for Detailed PTSD-analyses

Impact of Event Scale (IES by Horowitz et al., 1982, the 15-version). Intrusive thoughts and the compulsion to avoid situations that remind one of the trauma constitutes "thought terror" which is central to the suffering in a PTSD reaction. The IES scale examines these conditions on a broader basis. Due to the scale's international distribution, there are possibilities in comparing the results with other patient groups who have contracted PTSD injuries. The scale is found in different versions, varying in the number of items. We used a version with seven questions about intrusive thoughts (intrusion) and eight questions about avoiding behaviour (avoidance). This version is most often used in the Scandinavian and Anglo-Saxon world. The

TABLE 3
Strain Period in Number of Months and by Sex
(N = 61; 3 drop offs)

Number of Months	Total (N = 61)		Men (N = 19)	Women (N = 42)
0–11	9	(15%)	11%	17%
12–24	10	(16%)	21%	14%
25–48	12	(20%)	21%	19%
49–96	21	(34%)	32%	36%
97+	9	(15%)	16%	14%

evaluation is made in such a way that the answers "almost every day" and "at least once a week" each receive one point and answers "at least once a month" and "more seldom or never" receive no points. The instrument contains two scales. One measures "intrusion", i.e. intrusive recollections. The other measures "avoidance", i.e. the tendency to avoid situations that initiate memories.

Table 4 shows that 81% of our examined patients replied "almost every day" or "at least once a week" and thereby receive six or maximal seven points on "intrusion". The median lies around six points. Table 5 shows the "avoidance" aspect. The median lies—according to the same scale calculation as in Table 4—at five points; 67% of the examined patients received four, five, or six points. This means that it is very difficult for the patients to "turn off" the intrusive thoughts and that these, on the whole, constitute "thought terror" which they most often find themselves exposed to. The values in the Tables 4 and 5 must be regarded as extremely high.

Sleep and Alertness (The Caroline Institute Sleep Laboratory).   With few exceptions, the patients consistently had sleep problems. Table 6 shows a frequency distribution for 13 symptoms regarding sleep disturbances. The symptoms asked about were: difficulty in falling asleep; difficulty in awakening; waking up often during the night with difficulties in going to asleep; nightmares; not being thoroughly rested in the morning; final awakening too early; disturbed and uneasy sleep; tiredness during the day; eye irritations; dozing off during the day; being mentally tired during the day. Only the answers regarding "every day and or night" and "at least once a week" are included in Table 6, where only the highest frequencies (over 60% of the patients answered yes) are presented.

TABLE 4
IES: The Strength in "Intrusion" (*N* = 64)

Scale Points	Number of Answers	%	% Cumulative
0	1	1.6	1.6
1			1.6
2			1.6
3	5	7.8	9.4
4	1	1.6	11.0
5	5	7.8	18.8
6* **	24	37.5	56.3
7***	28	43.8	100.0

* = first quartile; ** = median; *** = third quartile.
No significant differences between genders were found.

TABLE 5
IES: The Strength in "Avoidance" (*N* = 64)

Scale Points	Number of Answers	%	% Cumulative
0	1	1.6	1.6
1	2	3.1	4.7
2	2	3.1	7.8
3	4	6.3	14.1
4*	11	17.2	31.3
5**	19	29.7	61.0
6***	13	20.3	81.3
7	5	7.8	89.1
8	7	10.9	100.0

* = first quartile; ** = median; *** = third quartile.
No significant differences between genders were found.

Furthermore, at least *30% of the patients* had the following difficulties *every night or day*: difficulty in falling asleep (33%); not being thoroughly rested in the morning (36%); disturbed or uneasy sleep (33%); tired during the day (33%); mentally tired during the day (36%).

Beck's Depression Inventory (BDI by Beck et al., 1961, the 13-version). The scale is found in different versions which vary in the number of questions asked. We used a version with 13 questions which is used most often in the Scandinavian and Anglo-Saxon world, thus allowing comparison. The response scales contains four categories. The first refers to a normal, non-depressive life situation (which gives 0 grade points). The other categories

TABLE 6
Sleep Problems from Which at Least 60% of the Patients
Suffered (*N* = 64)

Problem	% of Patients Answering Yes
Tired during the day	74
Difficulty in falling asleep	72
Mentally tired during the day	70
Not thoroughly rested in the morning	69
Often waking up during the night without being able to fall asleep again	67
Disturbed and uneasy sleep	66
Final awakening too early	61

(1 to 3) refer to increasingly severe depressiveness. The total score for the 13 items can thus vary between 0 and 39. Depression in connection with PTSD in this study only rarely scores higher than 25 points, which characterizes a very strong depression.

For an individual without a depression, this scale shows an average score of three to five. Values between six and 10 can be regarded as light depression, over 10 as moderate depression, and severe depression from 16 points.

Table 7 shows the frequencies for the 64 studied patients; 33% had a moderate depression while 39% suffered more severe states of illness such as would demand medical treatment.

Two Comprehensive Diagnoses

Post-traumatic Symptom Scale (PTSS-10 by Malt; Raphael et al., 1989). This questionnaire can be used separately as a screening instrument. The 10 questions are presented to individuals who have been subjected to various traumatizing events. The answers to the 10 questions alone do not reveal whether the individual has a PTSD reaction, but the answers do reveal whether the individual should be subject to further extensive diagnostical follow-up.

In our diagnosis, this instrument is used as one of the first, since it offers *both* the evaluator *and* the patient an initial, plausible survey of the problem. The answers also give rise to immediate semitherapeutic conversations.

Table 8 shows that more than half of the patients (57%) gave eight or more out of 10 possible yes answers. Thus, this patient group lies statistically at a very high response level. In total, 78% gave six or more yes answers. Only 6% of the patients had less than three yes answers.

PTSD Original Diagnosis (according to *DSM-III-R*, American Psychiatric Association, 1987).   The diagnosis of PTSD, post-traumatic stress disorder, was reached in 59 of the 64 patients. The remaining five were

TABLE 7
The Degree of Depression According to Beck's BDI,
in Total and Gender Differences (N = 64)

Depression Degree	Total (%)	Men (%)	Women (%)
0–5	13	15	11
6–10	16	20	14
11–15	33	30	34
16–20	28	10	36
21–25	9	20	5
26+	2	5	–

TABLE 8
Distribution of Responses to PTSS-10 Questions
(N = 63, 1 drop out)

Scale Points	Number of Answers	%	% Cumulative
0	1	1.6	1.6
1	–	–	1.6
2	2	3.2	4.8
3	1	1.6	6.4
4	4	6.3	12.7
5	6	9.5	22.2
6*	5	7.9	30.1
7	8	12.7	42.8
8**	18	28.6	71.4
9***	8	12.7	84.1
10	10	15.9	100.0

* = first quartile; ** = median; *** = third quartile.
No significant differences between genders were found.

suffering from a burnout syndrome and were treated accordingly. For diagnosis criteria A the 59 patients diagnosed as having a PTSD had all been subjected to a series of traumatic experiences such as were revealed through the occupational social anamneses. For diagnosis criteria B the traumatic event is repeatedly relived in at least one of the following ways:

1. Returning, insistent and painful memories of the event.
2. Returning nightmares about the event.
3. Acting or feeling as if the event were repeated.
4. Intensive psychological discomfort from events that symbolize the trauma.

According to *DSM-III-R*, the patient should have had at least one of these four symptoms for intrusive thoughts ("though terror"); 39% of the patients had three such symptoms, 37% had all four (see Table 9).

For diagnostic criteria C the individual constantly avoids trauma associated stimuli or shows a general blunting of ability to react emotionally, as is revealed in at least three of the following criteria:

1. Efforts to avoid thoughts or feelings that are associated to the trauma.
2. Efforts to avoid activities or situations that awaken memories.
3. Inability to remember some important aspect of the trauma.
4. Marked reduction of interest for important activities.
5. Feeling of a lack of interest in or expulsion by others.

TABLE 9
Number of Reported Symptoms Amongst
the PTSD Criteria B (*N* = 59)

Number of Symptoms	Number of Patients	%
0	1	2
1	3	5
2	10	17
3	23	39
4	22	37

6. Limited affects.
7. A feeling of not having any future.

According to *DSM-III-R*, the patient shall have at least three of seven listed symptoms of situation-avoiding behaviour for the purpose of escaping the "thought terror". The 59 patients had an average of five such symptoms; 51% had at least six symptoms (see Table 10).

For diagnosis criteria D permanent signs of an over-reacting state are shown with at least two of the following symptoms:

1. Difficulty in falling asleep or uneasy sleep.
2. Irritability or burst of fury.
3. Concentration difficulties.
4. Tense vigilance.
5. Exaggerated reaction to unexpected external stimuli.
6. Physiological reactions in the presence of events that symbolize or are similar to the traumatic event.

TABLE 10
Number of Stated Symptoms Amongst
the PTSD Criteria C (*N* = 59)

Number of Symptoms	Number of Patients	%
1	1	2
2	3	5
3	5	8
4	3	5
5	17	29
6	26	44
7	4	7

According to *DSM-III-R*, the patient shall have at least two of the six psychosomatic symptoms. On average, the 59 patients had four such symptoms; 27% had all six (see Table 11).

Diagnosis criteria E is the patient's average strain period. The strain period during which the patient had been subjected to mobbing was very long. According to *DSM-III-R*, a symptom period of one month following the trauma suffices. For our patients, the strain period is estimated from the time that the patient's psychosocial working environment has become mentally intolerable and trauma has arisen (for a chronological description of the phases in the process, see Leymann, 1992b and this issue).

In Table 3 one can see that only 15% of the patients had a strain period of less than one year. Just as many, namely 15%, had a strain time exceeding eight years. Most of the patients, 70%, had a strain time of between two and eight years. There was no difference between men and women.

Differential Diagnostics

The third group of diagnostical instruments focuses on the differential diagnostics. PTSD in chronic or semichronic form seldom appears in isolation. Anxiety is of course a constantly present symptom. If anxiety becomes more accentuated, a predominance is commonly found either in the phobic anxietal area or in the area of panic or hysterical anxiety. PTSD is commonly found with a psychosomatic predominance (in such cases we compare with the GAD criteria D; see previous description in order to differentiate between the three types of somatic symptoms). Further predominance may be found for depression or its opposite, obsession.

Psychotic Tendencies.   Since PTSD patients often are incorrectly diagnosed, whereby they are given diagnoses in psychotic areas, we check for extreme manic physical movements (manirismus and posturismus);

TABLE 11
Number of Stated Symptoms in the PTSD
Criteria D (*N* = 59)

Number of Symptoms	Number of Patients	%
1	3	5
2	8	14
3	6	10
4	13	22
5	13	22
6	16	27

megalomania; hallucinations and extreme thought contents (paranoia). *None* of our patients thus far have shown signs of psychotic tendencies.

Middlesex Hospital Questionnaire, 40-version (Sidney, 1974).   Using this inventory, questions are asked concerning different tendencies that can reveal psychiatric charges in the following six areas: anxietal disposition, phobic disposition and/or social malfunction, obsessive disposition, psychosomatic disposition, depressive disposition, and disposition for anxietal hysteria and/or panic anxiety.

Table 12 shows the frequencies for these six conditions that can give scores of between 0 (no affirmative answer) and 8 (maximal number of affirmative answers). Four of the 64 patients could not be examined for various reasons.

Table 12 demonstrates that anxiety, psychosomatic problems, and depression are the secondary diagnoses most commonly found in PTSD patients. This should be seen as a very logical outcome in regard to the character of the items that constitute the PTSD syndrome.

Brief Psychiatric Rating Scale (BPRS by Overall and Gorham; Beller & Overall, 1984; Overall & Beller, 1984).   This diagnosis is carried out on the basis of three goals. Perhaps the most important one occurs from a differential diagnostical perspective in order to determine if the patient shows psychotic elements. Among the 64 patients examined, *not one* showed such elements in agreement with general clinical, catastrophic psychiatric observations: PTSD does not result in psychoses other than in very extreme exceptions.

For the second part, the patient makes his or her own judgement on the same scale as the diagnoser. Both judgements are compared. If there is a

TABLE 12
Middlesex Hospital Questionnaire: Six Anxiety Items
Measuring 1 (Lowest) to 8 (Highest) Points ($N = 64$): The First
Quartile, Median, and Third Quartile ($N = 60$)

Anxiety Item	First Quartile	Median	Third Quartile
Anxiety	3	5	6
Phobia	1	2	4
Obsession	2	4	4
Psychosomatic	3	5	6
Depression	3	5	7
Hysteria	1	2	3

No significant differences between genders were found.

high degree of agreement, it is assumed that the patient has good self and illness insights which are included in the other diagnostical instruments used. *All* patients showed a very good self-insight.

The third goal is to gain an additional basis for a differential judgement. It is these judgements that are statistically accounted for here. During the classification, we proceeded along the instruments's seven scale steps, where step 1 indicates "none", steps 2 and 3 "low value", steps 4 and 5 a "medium value", and steps 6 and 7 a "high value". In Table 13, the percentual distribution for only medium and high values are presented. Seven patients were not tested for various reasons.

Measurement of Remaining Life Quality

General Health Questionnaire (GHQ by Goldberg, 20-version; Goldberg, 1985; Goldberg & Williams, 1988). Due to the scale's international distribution, it is possible to compare results with other patient groups who have contracted PTSD injuries. The scale exists in different versions which vary in the number of questions asked. We used the version with 20 questions. This version is most often used in the Scandinavian and Anglo-Saxon world. The evaluation is made in such a way that the answers "worse than earlier" and "much worse than earlier" receive one point and the answers "more or less than earlier" and "better than earlier" receive 0

TABLE 13
Psychiatric Judgement of 16 Psychiatric Conditions in 57 Patients

Condition	Number of Patients with Value >4	Level 4/5 Medium Difficulties	Level 6/7 Severe Conditions
1. Somatical engagement	29	32%	19%
2. Anxiety	57	30%	70%
3. Emotionally reserved	33	54%	3%
4. Conceptional disorder	43	26%	49%
5. Guilt feelings	28	32%	17%
6. Tensions	48	60%	24%
7. Manirismus	0	0%	0%
8. Megalomania	0	0%	0%
9. Depressive mood	54	60%	35%
10. Irritability	10	17%	0%
11. Suspiciousness	23	37%	3%
12. Hallucinations	1	2%	0%
13. Motoric retardation	27	47%	0%
14. Collaboration difficulties	7	12%	0%
15. Paranoid thoughts	1	2%	0%
16. Lowered affect	43	70%	5%

points. The scores can thus lie between 0 as the lowest and 20 as the highest number of points. The maximal number of points indicates the worst remaining quality of life.

The median of the results for 62 patients lies at an extremely high 18 points and the third quartile lies at the maximum of 20. In total, 75% of the patients have values higher than 16. Only 8% lie under 10, which may be considered high in this connection. Only four patients have 1 or 0 points. This is shown in Table 14.

DISCUSSION

How Serious are Psychological Problems after Mobbing?

If the degree of difficulty in the diagnoses that our patients have received were compared with, for example, individuals who have run over and killed suicidal persons on railway lines (Malt, Karlehagen, & Leymann, 1993) or subway tracks (Theorell, Leymann, Jodko, Konarski, & Norbeck, 1994), we see pronounced differences. In general, people seem to be able intuitively to imagine how it must feel to try to brake a train of hundreds of tons of weight and how it is, despite these desperate efforts, to finally run over the person who has laid him- or herself on the tracks in order to die. Never-

TABLE 14
General Quality of Life According to Judgement of
20 Items (N = 62, 2 drop outs). Eight scale points
(2–7, 10, 12) received 0 value; these are not depicted

Scale Points	Number of Answers	%	% Cumulative
01	2	3.2	3.2
08	1	1.6	4.8
09	2	3.2	8.0
11	2	3.2	11.2
13	1	1.6	12.8
14	3	4.8	17.6
15*	3	4.8	22.4
16	1	1.6	24.0
17	5	8.1	32.1
18**	11	17.8	49.9
19	7	11.3	61.2
20***	24	38.7	100.0

* = first quartile; ** = median; *** = third quartile.
No significant differences between genders were found.

theless, the driver's PTSD reaction is—statistically seen—very much milder than that of our patients, Also, a considerably smaller proportion of train drivers suffer a PTSD reaction and share the severe PTSD diagnoses. Indeed the number is very small in comparison with the condition which prevails for patients such as ours, who almost all receive severe diagnoses. This comparison might illustrate what the latter group of patients must have gone through in terms of psychological pain, anxiety, degradation, and helplessness—leading to such extensive PTSD injuries. Our patients can, on the other hand, in their reactions be compared with those accounted for in a Norwegian study concerning raped women (Dahl, 1989).

As a comparison to the high outcome of the PTSD degree, it may be of interest to mention what the investigation of Swedish and Norwegian train drivers revealed, after they had run over and killed suicidal individuals on the tracks: The frequency of high "intrusion"—and "avoidance"—values (Tables 4 and 5) were *considerably lower* than in the present study (Malt et al., 1993). Even a study that mapped psychological problems in subway drivers in Stockholm shows a *considerably lower* frequency of drivers with psychological problems after having run over suicidal individuals on the tracks (Theorell et al., 1994). The previously mentioned study of raped women shows very high values on the two IES scales (Dahl, 1989). We recommend as a hypothesis that high IES-values are present if the traumatic event is followed by a series of further traumatizing rights violations and identity insults from different societal sources (Leymann, 1989). This did not occur in the groups of engine drivers but it did occur in cases of raped women—and, of course, in the mobbed employees in question in the present study. Mobbing and expulsion from the labour market *are in themselves* a series of victimizations of traumatic strength.

Our present hypothesis is that PTSD takes on a much worse development if the traumatic situations last a long period of time *and* are followed by rights violations over a long period, such as caused by the judicial system or within the health-care community. Leymann (1989) carried out a large review of the literature in respect to catastrophic psychiatry and victimology based on about 25,000 pages of scientific victimological text in order to make an inventory of such disappointments, insults, and renewed traumas following an introductory "causal trauma"—a trauma which thereafter leads to, due to society's structure and functional ways, what is called "traumatizing consequential events". Many of these are provoked by the way that administrative instances deal with or abstain from dealing with the situation.

The mobbed employee who has become our patient suffers from a *traumatic environment*: psychiatrists, social insurance offices, the personnel department, managers, co-workers, the labour union, doctors in general practice, or company health care, etc., can if events so progress, produce worse and worse traumata.

Thus, our patients, like raped women, find themselves under a continuing threat. As long as the perpetrator is free, the woman can be attacked again. As long as the mobbed individual does not receive effective support, he or she can, at any time, be torn to pieces again.

In this manner, these individuals find themselves in both a prolonged stress-creating and a prolonged trauma-creating situation. Instead of a short, acute (and normal!) PTSD reaction that can subside after several days or weeks, theirs is constantly renewed: Additional new trauma and new sources of anxiety occur in a constant stream during which time the individual experiences rights violations that further undermine his or her self-confidence and psychological health. The unwieldy social situation for these individuals consists thus, not only of severe psychological trauma but, moreover, of an extremely prolonged stress condition that seriously threatens the individual's socio-economical existence. Torn out of their social network, a life of early retirement with permanent psychological damage threatens the great majority of mobbing victims.

ACKNOWLEDGEMENTS

Heinz Leymann assumed responsibility for collecting the data (the diagnoses) and writing the report. Anneli Gustafsson was responsible for processing the data and statistics. I would like to thank Dr Sue Baxter for her great help with the translation and Dr J. Knispel for his research language advice (Research Language Advice, 22303 Hamburg, Mühlenkamp 8D).

REFERENCES

Adams, A. (1992). *Bullying at work*. London: Virago Press.

Arbetarskyddsstyrelsens Författnings Samling. (1993). *Kränkande särbehandling i arbetslivet [Victimization at work]* (Vol. 17). Stockholm: Arbetarskyddsstyrelsen.

Arbetarskyddsstyrelsens Författnings Samling. (1994). *Arbetsanpassning och rehabilitering [Work assignment and vocational training]* (Vol. 1). Stockholm: Arbetarskyddsstyrelsen.

American Psychiatric Association. (1987). *Diagnostic and statistical manual of mental disorders (DSM-III-R)* (rev. 3rd ed.). Washington DC: Author.

Beck, A.T., Ward, Mendelsohn, Mock, & Erbaugh. (1961). An inventory for measuring depression. *Archives of General Psychiatry, 4*, 561–571.

Becker, M. (1993). Mobbing—ein neues Syndrom [Mobbing—a new syndrome]. *Spektrum der Psychiatrie und Nervenheilkunde, 22*, 108–110.

Beller, S.A., & Overall, J.E. (1984). The brief psychiatric rating scale (BPRS) in geropsychiatric research: II. Representative profile patterns. *Journal of Gerontology, 39*(2), 194–200.

Dahl, S. (1989). Acute response to rape—a PTSD variant. *Acta Psychiatrica Scandinavia, 80* (Suppl. 355), 56–62.

Einarsen, S., & Raknes, B.I. (1991). *Mobbing i arbeidslivet. En undersökelse av forekomst ol helsemessige av mobbing på norske arbeidsplasser [Mobbing in worklife: A study on prevalence and health effects of mobbing in Norwegian workplaces]*. Bergen: Forskningssenter for arbeidsmiljö (FAHS).

Goldberg, D. (1985). Identifying psychiatric illness among general medical patients. *British Medical Journal, 291*, 161–162.

Goldberg, D., & Williams, P. (1988). *A user's guide to the general health questionnaire*. Windsor, UK: NFER-Nelson.

Holen, A. (1990). *A long-term outcome study of survivors from a disaster*. Oslo: University of Oslo.

Horowitz, M.J., Wilner, & Alvarez. (1982). Impact of event scale: A measure of subjective distress. *Psychosomatic Medicine, 41*, 207–218.

Leymann, H. (1986). *Vuxenmobbning—om psykiskt våld i arbetslivet [Mobbing—psychological violence at work places]*. Lund: Studentlitteratur.

Leymann, H. (1988). *Ingen annan utväg [No way out]*. Stockholm: Wahlström & Widstrand.

Leymann, H. (1989). *När livet slår till [When life strikes]*. Stockholm: Natur och Kultur.

Leymann, H. (1990). *Handbok för användning av LIPT-formuläret för kartläggning av risker för psykiskt våld arbetsmiljön [The LIPT questionnaire—a manual]*. Stockholm: Violen.

Leymann, H. (1992a). *Vuxenmobbning på svenska arbetsplatser. En rikstäckande undersökning med 2.428 intervjuer [Mobbing at Swedish work places—a study of 2428 individuals: Frequencies]*. (Delrapport 1 om frekvenser.) Stockholm: Arbetarskyddsstyrelsen.

Leymann, H. (1992b). *Från mobbning till utslagning i arbetslivet [From mobbing to expulsion in work life]*. Stockholm: Publica.

Leymann, H. (1992c). *Manligt och kvinnligt vid vuxen mobbning. En rikstäckande undersökning med 2.428 intervjuer [Gender and mobbing—a study of 2428 individuals]*. (Delrapport 2.) Stockholm: Arbetarskyddsstyrelsen.

Leymann, H. (1992d). *Psykiatriska hälsoproblem i samband med vuxenmobbning. En rikstäckande undersökning med 2,428 intervjuer [Psychiatric problems after mobbing—a study of 2428 individuals]*. (Delrapport 3.) Stockholm: Arbetarskyddsstyrelsen.

Leymann, H. (1992e). *Lönebidrag och mobbad. En svag grupps psykosociala arbetsvilkor i Sverige [The psychosocial work conditions of a group of handicapped workers in Sweden]*. Stockholm: Arbetarskyddsstyrelsen.

Leymann, H. (Ed.). (1995). *Der neue Mobbing-Bericht [The new mobbing report]*. Reinbek: Rowohlt.

Leymann, H., & Gustafsson, A. (in press). *Sjuksystrarnas suicider*.

Leymann, H., & Gustavsson, B. (1984). *Psykiskt våld i arbetslivet. Två explorativa undersökningar [Psychological violence at work places: Two explorative studies]*. (Undersökningsrapport 42.) Stockholm: Arbetarskyddsstyrelsen.

Leymann, H., & Lindroth, S. (1993). *Vuxenmobbning mot manliga förskollärare [Mobbing of male teachers at kindergartens]*. Stockholm: Arbetarskyddsstyrelsen.

Leymann, H., & Tallgren, U. (1989). Undersökning av frekvensen vuxenmobbning inom SSAB [A study of mobbing frequencies at SSAB]. *Arbete, människa, miljö, 1*, 110–115.

Malt, U. (1989). The validity of the general health questionnaire in a sample of accidentally injured adults. *Acta Psychiatrica Scandinavia, 80*(355), 103–112.

Malt, U., Karlehagen, J., & Leymann, H. (1993). The effect of major railway accidents on the psychological health of train drivers: II. A longitudinal study of the one-year outcome after the accident. *Journal of Psychosomatic Research, 8*(37), 807–817.

Niedl, K. (1995). *Mobbing/Bullying am Arbeitsplatz [Mobbing/bullying at the work place]*. München: Rainer Hampp Verlag.

Olweus, D. (1993). *Bullying at school: What we know and what we can do*. Oxford: Blackwell.

Overall, J.E., & Beller, S.A. (1984). The brief psychiatric rating scale (BPRS) in geropsychiatric research: I. Factor structure on an inpatient unit. *Journal of Gerontology, 39*, 187–193.

Paanen, T., & Vartia, M. (1991). *Mobbing at workplaces in state government* (in Finnish). Helsinki: Finnish Work Environment Fund.

Pallechi, D., Nicolau, Biagi, & Nardini. (1990). The Middlesex Hospital questionnaire (MHQ) compared with the MMPI: Study of internal and reciprocal correlations between the psychodiagnostic scales. *Medicina Psicosomatica, 35*(3), 167–175.

Raphael, B., Lundin, T., & Weisaeth, L. (1989). A research method for the study of psychological and psychiatric aspects of disaster. *Acta Psychiatrica Scandinavia, 80*(353).

Sidney, C. (1974). The Middlesex Hospital questionnaire (MHQ) in clinical research: A review. In Pichot & Olivier-Martin (Eds.), *Psychological measurements in psychopharmacology*. Basel: S. Karger.

Svenska statens statistika årsbok [The Swedish government's statistical year book]. (1994).

Theorell, T., Leymann, H., Jodko, M., Konarski, K., & Norbeck, H.E. (1994). "Person under train" incidents from the subway driver's point of view: A prospective one-year follow-up study: The design, and medical and psychiatric data. *Social Science and Medicine, 38*, 471–475.

World Health Organization. (1992). *International Classification of Diseases* (10th ed.) (*ICD-10*). Göttingen: Huber.

Zilberg, N.J., Weiss, & Horowitz, M.J. (1982). The evaluation of IES. *Journal of Consulting and Clinical Psychology, 50*(3), 407–414.

EUROPEAN JOURNAL OF WORK AND ORGANIZATIONAL PSYCHOLOGY, 1996, 5 (2), 277–294

A Case Study of Mobbing and the Clinical Treatment of Mobbing Victims

Dieter Groeblinghoff and Michael Becker

Brandenburg Clinic of Psychosomatics, Neubrück, Berlin

This article documents two cases describing aspects of an integrated concept on overall and clinical (means of) diagnostics of mobbing victims suffering from psychological/psychosomatic diseases. Mobbing can cause severe illness, occupational and earning disability, social exclusion, and even suicide. It frequently generates chronic syndromes of combined psycho-physical disorders, restricting and impairing the afflicted persons. As a consequence of mobbing, even after a relatively short period of time a post-traumatic stress disorder (PTSD) can be diagnosed. Later (after about one to two years) a general anxiety disorder (GAD) can evolve. After further chronic progress severe, mainly depressive and/or obsessive syndromes regularly develop. At this stage the personality of the afflicted person is prone to profound and irreversible alteration. We use adapted techniques of anamnesis, especially the differentiated description and analysis of working conditions, supported by a combination of well-documented psycho- and sociometric instruments. The therapy programme for our clinic ranges from six to eight weeks, depending on individual aetiology, characteristics of prevalent syndromes, and therapy response. It is supplementing or replacing ambulant prophylaxis and therapy, as well as the obligatory ambulant aftercare.

INTRODUCTION

Mobbing was first investigated by Leymann (Leymann & Gustavsson, 1984) who presented the LIPT-questionnaire (Leymann, 1990) and who carried out several studies between 1985 and 1992 (see Leymann, this issue). Other studies were conducted, e.g. in Austria (Niedl, 1995), Finland (Paanen & Vartia, 1991), Germany (Becker, 1993; Groeblinghoff, 1994; Knorz & Zapf, 1996; Zapf, Knorz, & Kulla, this issue), Norway (Einarsen & Raknes, 1991), also in Australia, Denmark, and USA. Leymann (1993) suggested an operational definition of mobbing which was elaborated as the current definition by the international Association Against Psychological Stress and Mobbing (GPSM) in 1993 (see later). According to this definition mobbing

Requests for reprints should be addressed to D. Groeblinghoff, Ludwigstrasse 34B, D-70176 Stuttgart, Germany. Email: +49-791855102.0001@t-online.de

actions should occur often, repeatedly, and systematically (statistically, at least for half a year and once a week), within equal or unequal power structures, aimed at a certain person who experiences this as a discrimination (see also Leymann, this issue). An important fact was that Leymann found a post-traumatic stress syndrome (PTSD) occurring with nearly half of the examined victims (Leymann & Gustafsson, this issue).

As a complex and, according to common standards of human rights, unethical disorder of communication and an extreme psychosocial stressor, mobbing is frequently causing severe syndromes of combined psychological and physical illness. The tendency to chronic progression is considerably restricting and narrowing the afflicted persons in their spectrum of vitality. It heavily impairs their overall potential and creativity, and their productivity at work. Mobbing can lead quickly to the loss of individual health resources and coping mechanisms, particularly so if alternatives are lacking (e.g. change of work place) or if additional problems in private life are involved (cf., e.g., Lazarus & Folkman, 1984). This can finally result in dismissal from work, occupational and earning disability, and in extreme cases and after long periods of illness in social exclusion, sometimes even in suicide. So, if not prevented, an ambulant and/or a clinical rehabilitative therapy can be required (Becker & Groeblinghoff, 1994).

Outside Scandinavia mobbing has been an issue of a wider public discussion only since 1992, so it was only then that people, particularly victims, became increasingly aware of this problem. For the first time their suffering could be traced back much more comprehensively to complex origins in the workplace. As patients they had reported their complaints long before, but from then on they had an increased chance of adequate diagnosis and treatment. Since there had been hardly any professional training, competent counselling or help was nearly impossible to find. So far no comprehensive clinical experience was available. How this reduced the possibilities of occupational rehabilitation, or even basic help and therapy (Leymann, 1993) is not too difficult to estimate.

An important step was that the first mobbing clinic could be opened in 1992 in Germany (Becker, 1993) in co-operation with Leymann. The clinic had treated approximately 100 patients when these experiences were transferred to the Swedish clinic's advantage in 1994. Another meaningful step in Germany was made in spring 1993 with the foundation of the "Gesellschaft gegen psychosozialen Stress und Mobbing e.V. GPSM" (Association Against Psychosocial Stress and Mobbing). It was initiated by researchers working in this area (Leymann and the authors, among others), members of sociopolitical institutions (such as trade unions, the church, or communal health insurance organizations) active in this field, and physicians and psychologists. The GPSM is an international forum for research, qualified information (especially for professional helpers), and social support. Whereas this non-profit association is growing fast, with numerous members (and researchers) from neighbouring countries as well, the clinic's continuous work is unfortunately inhibited by the present restrictive social policy, despite the many reports of serious illnesses which have become public in recent years.

Being far behind the Swedish legislation, other countries have an even stronger need for studies on the damaging social and health effects of mobbing that underline the necessity of improvement measures.

In this article we present a case study to demonstrate several aspects of mobbing such as the long-term process and outcome of injuries and ill-health. It also illustrates the usually very complex setting of typical mobbing development, and interrelates discussion of the victim's, culprit's, or system's responsibility for mobbing (cf. e.g., the published case studies in Becker, 1995; Groeblinghoff, 1994; Leymann, 1993, 1995; Resch, 1994).

METHODS

From a clinical point of view it must be kept in mind that mobbing and the consequent damages to health represents a psychodynamic process. The examiner only selects the momentary, subjective setting. Care must therefore be taken not only in judgements reached but also in the proposals of intervention derived. A careful history taking as the primary basis for any other means of diagnostics can develop not only a first picture of the work situation but allows also a first impression of the victim's personality structure (after deformation by mobbing, cf. Leymann, this issue). Bearing in mind the limitations, a specific social anamnesis regarding mobbing enables the interviewer to differentiate within this process and to decide about further necessary examination instruments. The German and the Swedish clinics agree upon internationally well-documented catastrophic psychiatric diagnostic instruments as well as instruments measuring aspects of the organization (cf. Leymann & Gustafsson, this issue), of which the following three are presented in this article in more detail:

1. Zerssen Complaint List (Zerssen, 1971, self-judgement scale: 24 items of psychosomatic complaints according to their subjective intensity).

2. The Instrument for Stress-oriented Job Analysis, ISTA (Semmer & Dunckel, 1991; Semmer, Zapf, & Dunckel, in press; Zapf, 1993; self-report scales including job content variables, communication at work and work-related stressors); a scale of social stressors at work (Frese & Zapf, 1987) referring to the social climate in the work group, and conflicts with colleagues and supervisors; and a social support scale (Frese, 1989).

3. Leymann Inventory of Psychological Terrorization, LIPT (Leymann, 1990; German version, LIPT-II, Niedl, 1995), 45 mobbing actions of 5 categories, regarding: (a) contacts, (b) isolation, (c) tasks, (d) reputation, and (e) violation.

CASE STUDIES

The presentation of two cases, a man (Mr R.) and a woman (Mrs F.) in the same institution, being mobbed over a long time period partly by the same persons, is used to show how mobbing victims can be diagnosed and treated. Both have been examined within neurological-psychiatric expertise under the question of whether workplace related and psychosocial stressors may have caused, or contributed to, their diseases.

Mr R., Aged 56 Years

Anamnesis

In the general anamnesis and critical incident analysis, the family anamnesis showed no significant indications of a disordered development during childhood or adolescence, both of which Mr R. described as cheerful. He spent a major part of his school life in an extern college, finishing in 1961 with the high school/college diploma. Only disturbed sleep during the final examinations, which could be interpreted as an enhanced psychosomatic reaction, is worth remarking upon. Some accident-related and other physical complaints are not relevant to this mobbing discussion. Mr R. declared that he was never seriously ill except from in his present workplace environment. In particular he was always at full psychological capability. Later in his private life, he was divorced; otherwise there were no problems. He now is living with his new female partner who is 12 years younger than himself. His 19-year-old daughter is living with his ex-wife. Besides the symptoms mentioned in the tests (see later) he reported a secondary sedative abuse subsequent to prescriptions upon his mobbing-related problems, and the recent onset of suicidal thoughts and impulses simultaneous with registering the impending administrative tribunals.

The workplace and mobbing anamnesis of Mr R. showed, from the college-diploma on, a splendid career as a local government official, with employment at several county administrations and as the director of a community administration since 1974. The first 10 years of his career, under the then elected mayor, were very good, with just the normal interpersonal conflicts that occur in any organization. Consequently, the town council had honoured him with a unanimous nomination as the director of the community administration. He was also very successful in this position.

However, from 1984 on, which was the beginning of the governmental period of the then newly elected and still ruling mayor, his work situation became immediately, and increasingly, stressful. The normal conflicts of the former work situation turned into psychological violence against him. He was more and more harassed by the mayor, who from the beginning did not want to co-operate. This led to a prevalence of illness. In this process he was more and more isolated and cut off from vital information not only by the mayor but also by the town council. The situation had culminated so much that besides organizational measures even measures of criminal prosecution (which had to be dropped) were initiated against him. He was also obliged to see the medical officer to have a judgement made on his working capability. Moreover, the mayor was intending a disciplinary tribunal against him, aimed at expelling him from his status of an official.

Health Status

(Reported are the pathological findings relevant in the context of mobbing.) The general somatic and neurological status showed an upper and lower spinal syndrome, frequently to be found in conjunction with psychological stress and the subsequential chronical muscle hypertension. Signs of physical damage following the sedative abuse were not apparent.

Psychologically, the behaviour appeared correct, sometimes pedantic, with high aspirations regarding standards, laws, and morals. In this respect he sometimes seemed slightly anancastic, even obsessive, appearing as hypersensitive towards his surroundings, and permanently hyperactively adapting and deeply involving himself with the agonies and fates of others. Within the examinational situation he sometimes appeared impatient and aggressive, showing an overall hyperirritable attitude. Mr R. had been injured frequently in the past and had become very vulnerable. Therefore, he tended to interpret harmless interventions as afflictions. Generally, he appeared easily unsure of himself, unveiling desperate, anxious but also unprotected aspects of his personality. Based on a resigned, depressive attitude, indicated by hopelessness, he was still courageous and highly motivated, despite the enhanced psychological pressure he was obviously subjected to. As a result he reacted impulsively, was maladapted and inflexible, socially retreating too soon, and had an enhanced suspicious behaviour. He was internally restless with a generally lowered reagibility. He described his workplace problems very extensively, constantly appearing rather agitated. The single processes were described in detail, so the presentation gained the character of a monologue, thus making the situation as a whole difficult to understand for the interviewer. His thinking was continuously circling around the sufferings in his workplace, the memories repeatedly urging themselves into his mind (automatic thinking), thus getting the character of intrusions. Moreover, as his comprehensive interests in life, his sociability, and perception of emotions decreased, tendencies of alienation were appearing. During examination his alertness, concentration, and perception were widely intact. No mnestic, no contentious or formal cognitive, perceptional, or identity disturbances were apparent.

Testing Mr R. using the Zerssen complaint list (Zerssen, 1987), we found 18 symptoms to be severe (seven), medium severe (eight), or moderate (three), thus indicating a considerable psychological/psychosomatic problem. Psychologically prevalent were symptoms of agitation and blockage (automatically recurring thoughts, irritability, inner unrest, hyposomnia), physically such of distinct gastrointestinal (abdominal pain, stuffiness, obstipation), and musculosceletal disorders (lower back pain, upper back and shoulder pain with chronic muscle hypertension), further psychosomatic complaints (hyperperspiration, chest pain, feeling weak, heavy/weak but restless legs, dizziness, tremors).

Applying the instrument for stress-oriented job analysis (Semmer & Dunckel, 1991; Semmer et al., in press; Zapf, 1993) and the social stressors scale (Frese & Zapf, 1987) we found that, despite a low sick leave rate, stress levels were generally high with strong fluctuations, primarily caused by work organization, work environment, and social conditions, less by general organizational conditions; the tasks appeared stress-free. There was a high coincidence with the items named by Mrs F. (see later). Prevalent factors were, for example: personnel too few, legal rules abandoned, numerous complaints from colleagues, strong fluctuations, frequent disputes, quarrels and social conflicts, frequent or constant work under time pressure, frequent problems of co-operation, stress from the work environment. Moreover, difficulties between colleagues and with superiors (the mayor) were important, only very low chances of influencing organizational decisions were given.

Analysing the mobbing behaviour using the LIPT-II questionnaire (Leymann, 1990; Niedl, 1995), the most frequent actions occurring either daily or at least weekly over half a year were of the categories "contacts" and "isolation", less of "reputation", and none of "tasks" and "violation" (exception: hand-written addition "prone to be cast out by disapproval of competencies"). A high coincidence was found with answers of Mrs F. regarding the number and frequency of reported actions. Most of the mobbing behaviours lasted longer than five years. Prevalent mobbing actions were:

1. *Contacts*: inhibitions of articulating by superior but never by others; continuous interruptions by superior; continuous criticizing of work; devaluating, negative glances, or gestures without direct verbal ex-

pression; total isolation and obstruction of information; personnel split; no chance of reporting and discussing problems with the councils or committees;

2. *Isolation*: is not spoken to by others; not desired to speak to others; unofficial prohibition for colleagues to speak with him;
3. *Tasks*: disapproval of competencies;
4. *Reputation*: speaking badly of him behind his back; spreading false rumours about him and making him look ridiculous in front of others; work judged in a wrong and harmful manner; his decisions are questioned;
5. *Violence*: none.

All actions against him were considered to be equally serious. The opponents were both colleagues, subordinates, and superiors; amongst them both men and women. He received only private support by friends, relatives, and others (e.g. his physicians).

Interpretation

The explanations of Mr R. can, of course, not be considered as facts but as the diagnostically and therapeutically traceable interpretations and descriptions of the examinee (patient). The basic (but unresolved) conflict may have originated in the different opinions of the elected mayor (a former computer retailer) and the administration professional regarding the primary tasks of the administrative authority and how they should be carried out. The consequence of this conflict was the demonstration of omnipotence by the mayor, and the over-reactive behaviour of Mr R., without finding substantial and constructive solutions to organize the work. In the course of the quarrels a social incompetence of the authority as a whole (including the mayor) was being unveiled, even its inability to recognize the constructive and innovative potential of fairly resolved conflicts at work. Hence a mobbing process could develop. Because the situation did not change, for instance by the election of another mayor or by the opportunity of another comparable job for Mr R. as a way out, he became more and more desperate. In the course of time the possibilities to act decreased, producing all the administrative and health-destroying consequences of lost control. In the early stages, the elimination of Mr R. might have been just a wish, later it was the strong intention of at least the mayor. In the final stage many things merged into a malignant dead-end: e.g. the secondary and partial—at least to the extent of prescribing drugs instead of aiming at a comprehensive solution of health problems—iatrogenic sedative abuse, an impending administrative tribunal, and the persisting humiliation of the threat of early retirement because of professional failure. Such a combination must be taken particularly seriously in this final stage of personnel administrative measures, with Mr R. facing the onset of suicidal thoughts and impulses (cf. Leymann, 1987).

The health consequences were: multiple psychosomatic complaints running parallel to a formerly rigid and resistant, but increasingly depressive, attitude with increasing and worsening suicidal thoughts and a permanent mental activation (automatic thoughts), and last but not least a secondary dependency syndrome. The symptoms were aggravating, both in quality and quantity, causing a deterioration of Mr R.'s health and personality.

Diagnosis

The diagnosis is based on the *International classification of diseases* (ICD-10; World Health Organization, 1992) and the *Diagnostic and statistical manual of mental disorders* (*DSM-III-R*; American Psychiatric Association, 1987) and the extensions and specifications of ICD and DSM of Leymann and Gustafsson (this issue), thus integrating the experiences in both the Swedish and the German clinic.

Mr R.'s syndrome contains numerous symptoms and a pattern to be found in the following wider description of *post-traumatic stress disorder* (PTSD). As a consequence of mobbing this diagnosis can be stated even after a rather short period of time (about ¼–½ year). Typical is the development of symptoms caused by a strain-causing event or process beyond the usual human experience (causing strain for nearly everyone), leading to intensive fear, shock, or helplessness. What is important is that mobbing is not only a singular straining event but a progressively worsening situation (Leymann, 1993). Thus, the intensity of the PTSD caused by mobbing is incomparably stronger than that caused by a singular straining event, for instance witnessing a fatal traffic accident.

Patients suffering from PTSD show symptoms such as sleeping disorders (start/continuity) often with recurring nightmares, hypervigilance, overwrought panic reactions, physical reactions being confronted with events resembling or symbolizing aspects of the traumatizing event, disorders of memory and concentration, tendencies towards aggressive reactions (as an irritability with the fear of losing control, and outbursts of aggression), inability to express anxiety. Typical are intrusions, i.e. continuously recurring recollections of traumatic aspects. The intensity of intrusions can range from images and scenes of the traumatizing situation rising in front of the inner eye through to dissociative phenomena, where the patients have the impression of actually being back in the situation itself, and no longer being able to differentiate between imagination and memory.

The PTSD in this case was meanwhile transformed into a *persistent personality alteration*. As under the first diagnosis Mr R.'s symptoms can be clearly subsumed under the following extended description. After further chronification of PTSD, severe depressive or/and obsessive syndromes are regularly found. At this stage the personality has changed considerably. A persistent personality alteration can succeed the experience of extreme stress, for which the vulnerability of the afflicted person is not a sufficient explanation. An example of this could be the experience of a concentration camp.

To establish this diagnosis several of the following features have to be prevalent as was the case with Mr R.: a generalized hostile or distrustful attitude, social retirement, feelings of emptiness or hopelessness, chronic agitation. As apparent with constant, threatening alienation, the alteration should last at least two years, and not be primarily based on another disease. In order to survive, Mr R. would have to question his ideals. His previous attitude and behaviour, corresponding with his ideals and personality structure, were no longer protecting or supporting him sufficiently. Accordingly, behavioural changes resulted which led to a reconstruction of his personality as a whole. Therefore, instead of diagnosing his original personality, his destructed one—with often comparable symptomatics—can be recorded, so it seems to be misleading and unproven to assume that generally one or more certain types of personalities are prone to be affected by mobbing within this complex system (cf. Leymann, this issue).

With regard to his rather depressive expression, apart from the described features a chronic inability to feel any kind of joy at everyday little things and events was apparent. Moreover, there is his constant high risk of substance abuse (here: sedatives) and developing a secondary dependency syndrome. In a case of a prevalent obsessive superimposition there is additionally prevailing a hypersensitivity towards injustice, with a steadily present hyperactive acquisition and involvement in the fate of others (pathological, self neglect, social overengagement).

Mrs F., Aged 49 years

Anamnesis

The general anamnesis and critical incident analysis showed no signs of a significant disturbed childhood and adolescence. Although she described her father as a difficult person—who primarily made her mother suffer and had a minor influence on her—nevertheless she claimed not to have had an unhappy childhood. After high school she entered public administration. her training (with an extra specialization) and her first 10 years of working as the administative director of the construction authority were without unusual problems. Besides stress-related problems caused by her workplace she was never seriously ill. In particular, she always sustained her full psychological capability.

In her workplace and mobbing anamnesis Mrs F. described that in 1984 the newly elected mayor, in contrast to his predecessor, from the beginning had given her—as the director of the construction authority—orders without discussing the contents, sometimes orders not legally performable. This caused increasing conflict of conscience in her, resulting in her counselling the chairman of her administration, Mr R., particularly when the frequency of these occurrences increased. She was subjected to more and more intense assaults by the new mayor, resulting in the damaging consequences on her health described later. She became increasingly isolated within the community administration. For instance, her application for an enhanced budget for her authority was not decided upon for years. From 1993 she was not invited to the regular meetings of the board of construction and community services (although she was the director of the associated authority!) although this had been always the case for the last 20 years. Meanwhile the employees of the whole community administration were increasingly more inclined against her and she was excluded from social events (e.g. celebrations). Regarding her department she hardly got any necessary information from the mayor, thus being considerably inhibited in her work. Moreover, the mayor tried to undermine the elections of the personnel commission in order to prevent her re-election as the chairwoman. Meanwhile there was only written communication between them. The situation had escalated so much that (as with Mr R.) in addition to administrative measures even criminal proceedings (which had to be dropped) were initiated against her. She was urged to visit the medical officer to have her working capability checked. More than that, the mayor wanted to set up a disciplinary tribunal against her with the aim of forcing her out of her position.

Health Status

There were no relevant general pathological findings, particularly no signs of damage by substance abuse. Mrs F. described her workplace problems in detail, sometimes losing track into irrelevant single facts, making the events appear a little confused. Imposing in this respect was her high level of agitation. Also at other points her impatience and her tendency to an aggressive response was repeatedly apparent. At enhanced sensitivity she appeared hyperirritable. She seemed injured and desperate, at times even overcharged and helpless, unprotected, and anxious. Her overall reagibility was reduced. Emotionally, she seemed depressed, unstable, her face showing her suffering. She agreed she had suicidal thoughts. Her self-esteem seemed reduced. On enquiry she reported weak memory and decreasing concentration. During examination she was continuously aware and alert, her comprehensiveness did not appear limited. When calm she complained about early exhaustion, and reported a considerable inner unrest. Her thinking was circling around the injuries suffered at her workplace. She reported intrusions (automatic thoughts), unavoidably oppressive memories of events at her workplace, alienation, and loss of interests, of social activities, and of perceiving emotions. Contentious disorders of cognition and perception, as well as of identity, were not found.

Examining Mrs F. with the Zerssen complaint list (Zerssen, 1971), eight symptoms appeared as severe or medium severe (irritability, inner unrest, restless legs, hypersensitivity against coldness, dizziness, weakness, nausea, lower back pain), eight were moderate, indicating a psychological/psycho-somatic problem with moderate abdominal and musculoskeletal complaints, along with a distinctly prevalent agitated depressive and resigned attitude, and moderate cognitive disturbances.

Applying the instrument for stress-oriented job analysis (Semmer & Dunckel, 1991) and the social stressors scale (Frese & Zapf, 1987) we found that, despite a low sick leave rate, a generally high stress level was prevailing, released primarily by work organization, work surroundings, and social conditions, less by organizational environment conditions; the task is reported as stress-free. In all, there was a high coincidence with the answers of Mr R.

Analysing the mobbing behaviour using the LIPT-II questionnaire (Leymann, 1990; Niedl, 1995), the most frequent actions occurring either daily or at least weekly over half of a year were of the categories "contacts" and "isolation", less of "reputation", and none of "tasks" and "violation" (exception—hand-written addition: "prone to be cast out by disapproval of competencies"). A high coincidence was found with the answers of Mr R. Regarding the number and frequency of reported actions and their persistence this has to be considered as mobbing according to Leymann's definition. Similarly to Mr R., most of the actions against her lasted longer than five years.

Interpretation

As to the mobbing process, a high coincidence with Mr R. was apparent. Her search to discuss the situation with him (as a co-victim and a supervisor at the same time) turned out to be rather devastating for Mrs F. A stigmatizing and aggravating point was perhaps her nomination as the chair-woman of the personnel commission.

It is obvious that mobbing caused severe illness in her case. Prevalent in the presented symptomatics were multiple psychosomatic complaints, e.g. inner unrest, generalized exhaustion, disorders of concentration, mnestics, sleep, intestinal functions, as well as facial pain and paresthesias in the extremities, running parallel to two to three years of depressive basic mood, with temporary, recently worsening, suicidal thoughts, and an almost permanent mental agitation (automatic thoughts) about the workplace stress put on her. The symptoms were aggravating in quality and quantity, going along with a deterioration of her health resources.

Diagnosis

Mrs F. was diagnosed as suffering from *post-traumatic stress disorder* (PSTD), with a secondary *dysthymous disorder*. As for the first diagnosis (and comparable to Mr R.) her symptoms are part of the generalized description given in this issue equal to and above the standards (cf. Leymann, this issue).

Mobbing can generate a profound, exaggerated, and unrealistic anxiety: that her life was threatened by the workplace situation and something bad or dangerous could happen to her immediately. After about one to two years a generalized anxiety disorder (GAD) can arise. It is usually combined with a diffuse state of physical tension, vegetative hyperirritability, and hypervigilance. She would be permanently busy with these thoughts, and finally realize her environment as hostile and frightening. Frequent are transitions into, or overlapping with, social phobia, which is related to the fear of doing something that could be submissive and devoting.

As a secondary consequence of a PTSD or a GAD a dysthymous disorder can be evoked. The cardinal symptom is her chronically depressive mood for most of the day, over more than half of all days, subjectively reported by her for at least two years. During this depressive mood at least two out of the following symptoms must be present, which was the case with Mrs F.: in/hyperappetence, hypo/hypersomnia, lack of energy, exhaustion, low self-esteem, low concentration, difficulties in making decisions, or hopelessness.

SUMMARY AND DISCUSSION

The cases of Mr R. and Mrs F. simultaneously represent both typical and extreme examples of victimization by mobbing. Regarding the workplace environment, they seemed to have had rather bad conditions, below average. A generally high stress level was prevailing, primarily caused by the work organization, work environment, and social conditions.

The cases seem worse than typical, with respect to the kind of numerous mobbing actions. All actions were reported as nearly equally serious. They confirm and illustrate the empirical results of Leymann (this issue), Niedl (1995), and Zapf et al. (this issue). The cases are certainly extreme in duration and with respect to the fact that we see two members of the upper management of a public administration mobbed by the same person. They were especially prone to mobbing because of the very high communicative and co-operative requirements of their jobs, and the increasing restriction of these and other basic requirements by a power-abusing but relatively ignorant supervisor, upon whom they became more and more dependent. The long persistence and the subsequent escalation of actions and consequences are extreme. Another special feature is the combination of these cases at one institution. Mr R., as an experienced rival, and Mrs F. as a "weak" but socially engaged woman, appeared as both a threat and a challenge for this more and more malignant mobber. Even harmonious collusion and mutual support of the victims could not be established. Additionally, different coping strategies, and a double witness of comparable mobbing situations developing into extremes, can be stated.

Considering the extremely long time of the mobbing process, the damage done to the victims' health represents an unfortunately rather typical outcome that we were often confronted with (cf. Becker, 1993; Groeblinghoff, 1994; Leymann, 1993, this issue). Psychologically prevalent were symptoms of depression, but also obsession, agitation and blockage, a resigned attitude, along with moderate cognitive disturbances, with automatically recurring thoughts, irritability, inner unrest, hyposomnia, substance abuse, and suicidal tendencies. Physical complaints referred to distinct gastro-intestinal (stuffed or narrow throat, gastro-abdominal pain, stuffiness, obstipation), and musculoskeletal disorders (back and shoulder pain with chronic muscle hypertension). Further psychosomatic complaints were, for example, hyperperspiration, chest pain, heavy, weak but restless legs, dizziness, tremors, hypersensitivity to the cold, weakness, and nausea. After a long period of coping, in one case with substance abuse, the final decompensation to suicidal tendencies is clearly at hand. In this acute and critical state of health, with their occupational and private perspectives deteriorated, the victims were not even able to search effectively for help by themselves.

The differential diagnostic question about their premorbid (more precisely: before mobbing) personalities can certainly not be answered to the last extent. Some conclusions can be derived from our descriptions and interpretations of each case. In our estimation both persons offered quite good conditions for their jobs, regarding their professional and social competencies, and in their social context. This can be underlined by the development of their careers before the new supervisor came, and, in contrast, how they declined since. In comparison, the distinct change in the workplace environment of these two independently successful individuals stresses the impact of prevalent systemic influences.

THERAPEUTIC ASPECTS

At this point some of our experiences and considerations regarding the background and establishment of an adequate, effective therapy and further support in cases like these two presented patients may be added (cf. Becker & Groeblinghoff, 1994; Groeblinghoff & Becker, 1995). Without a very careful job analysis, integrating the knowledge about the complex condition of mobbing, these patients face an often similar pattern of treatment. It is an individual- and symptom-oriented medical therapy, combined with (by wish of the patients) multiple sick leave, and often the prescription of psychopharmaceuticals. Despite well-meant intentions, an ongoing process of illness will result, as the basic aetiology has not sufficiently been considered, and therefore not referred to by adequate therapeutic measures (cf. Becker, 1993; Groeblinghoff, 1994). Under a continuously increasing psychological pressure psychosomatic or psychiatric clinic treatments are an almost inevitable consequence. If here the pathogenic impact of poor working conditions is ignored, too, misdiagnoses such as primary and prevalent personality disorders, or even paranoid psychoses and similar severe diseases, result. As a consequence, the treatment attempts are insufficient, illness prolonging, and in some cases even more damaging. This serious consequence of additional stigmatization (cf., e.g., Goffmann, 1967; Hohmeier, 1975) is strongly accelerating the social exclusion of the afflicted person, enhancing the suicidal thoughts and impulses which can often be observed in this stage. Therefore, an adequate ambulant and/or clinical treatment and rehabilitation has to be provided early enough (cf. Groeblinghoff, 1995).

Becker (1993) developed a clinical concept for mobbing victims in Bad Lippspringe, Germany, in co-operation with Leymann. The concept was further elaborated in 1994 for the Swedish Clinic (Leymann, 1995) and for the Brandenburg Clinic of Psychosomatics, Neubrück, Berlin (Becker & Groeblinghoff, 1994). An outline of the programme consisting of the major steps of treatment is summarized in the following.

1. Analysis

The therapy programme schedule at the clinic ranges from six to eight weeks depending on individual aetiology and therapy response. Admission to the clinic offers the primarily indicated stress-free and protective environment, and an integration into the therapeutic community. Rest and relaxation is intensified by appropriate techniques. The patients are enabled initially to accept their own fates, and being accordingly encouraged and motivated, to follow the course of the treatment. The first week is dedicated primarily to conscientious diagnostics, and to the elaboration of a therapy programme matching the patients' needs. Merely taking the social history seriously has a therapeutic effect as it is a very important opportunity for the afflicted person to report any subjectively meaningful facts without being interrupted or feeling neglected. The often complex events at work are first put into systematic order, with a transparent and reconstructable pattern of interaction. Next the organizational and working conditions, including management aspects, are examined, and the process of mobbing is thoroughly described. At this point less juridical reasoning, but much more logical and emotional comprehensiveness of the course of events is important. All this gives remarkable relief to the patients, who up to until then doubted more and more about themselves and struggled more or less vehemently against external condemnation. Supported by teaching material the new consciousness of the problem is then deepened and consolidated. At the same time the patients recognize their fates not to be singular and they identify peers. This is the first step to break free from constantly feeling guilty, to re-empower the inherent self-healing potential, and to rebuild a new self-esteem, stopping the thought-blocking internalized process of mobbing mentally. In particular they aim at the restitution of health and occupational capacity, and try to give up unrealistic goals of rehabilitation (e.g. using the clinical dismission report as a means of evidence in a court trial against the employer). The clinic will, together with the patients, elaborate practicable perspectives for their further occupational career.

2. Lysis

In the therapy groups of eight to ten persons, and in additional self-esteem stabilizing single sessions, typical mobbing behaviour is made transparent by different techniques of a pragmatic and systemic approach. Regarding aetiological conceptions and the aimed-for result (within a relatively compact time schedule: only short-term therapy is possible because of current legal restrictions) behaviour-oriented elements are preferred. Within this second therapy phase, by means of a special training programme for self-assurance blocking forms of behaviour are revealed and new kinds are taught. In addition, there are adapted sports- and motor-, as well as ergonomic-therapeutic and creativity-enhancing treatment units including physiotherapy.

3. Catharsis

As the relatives and close friends of the patients nearly always are deeply involved in the problem, they preferably should engage in the healing process as well; they should come into the clinic and participate in a programme of systemic therapy elements (cf., e.g., Ludewig, 1992; Stierlin, 1975). Here above all, the process of what has happened should be revealed to these persons, for their own relief too. In a second step new coping strategies for the future are worked out together. In case of the predictable loss of the old job (sometimes indicated even from a therapeutic point of view), new perspectives, e.g. a vocational rehabilitation programme, will be elaborated together. All patients are given the opportunity of specified juridical consultation concerning their mobbing situation. This intervention is agreed upon with the therapeutic team to ensure that the medical and juridical efforts are well co-ordinated. Here the main purpose is to show up realistic juridical perspectives and chances of eventual vocational rehabilitation (cf. Groeblinghoff, in press).

Finally it should be mentioned that the stationary clinical therapy must not be understood as an isolated intervention but explicitly includes prophylaxis and aftercare (cf. Ebeling, 1955; Halama, Möckel, & Gräntzdörffer, 1994, 1995; Leymann, 1993, 1995; Resch, 1994, 1995). Therefore continuous and close contact with the ever-expanding support network initiated by the GPSM (mentioned previously) is substantial.

REFERENCES

American Psychiatric Association. (1987). *Diagnostic and statistical manual of mental disorders (DSM III-R)* (rev. 3rd ed.). Washington DC: American Psychiatric Association.

Becker, M. (1993). Die stationäre Behandlung psychisch und psychosomatisch erkrankter Menschen aufgrund von Arbeitsplatsbelastungen [The clinical treatment of psychosomatic ill people due to workplace stress]. *Spektrum der Psychiatrie und Nervenheilkunde, 3*, 108–110.

Becker, M. (1995). Rückwege zum Selbstbewußtsein—Ein Beispiel für die Behandlung in der Mobbingklinik [Ways back to self-esteem—an example for the treatment in the mobbing clinic]. In H. Leymann (Ed.), *Der neue Mobbing Bericht. Erfahrungen und Initiativen—Auswege und Hilfsangebote* (pp. 124–144). Reinbek bei Hamburg: Rowohlt.

Becker, M., & Groeblinghoff, D. (1994). Rehabilitation of harassment victims who have psychiatric problems. In *Back to Work: Proceedings of the First International Conference on Vocational Rehabilitation, Work and Health Welfare* (pp. 119–123). Ronneby Brunn, Sweden: Ett Helt Liv & Swedish Federation of Social Insurance.

Ebeling, J. (1995). Ärztliche Hilfe in der ambulanten Praxis—Ein persönlicher Bericht [Medical help in the ambulant practice—a personal report]. In H. Leymann (Ed.), *Der neue Mobbing Bericht. Erfahrungen und Initiativen—Auswege und Hilfsangebote* (pp. 145–152). Reinbek bei Hamburg: Rowohlt.

Einarsen, S., & Raknes, B.I. (1991). *Mobbning i arbeitslivet. En undersökelse av forekomst ol helsemessige av mobbing på norske arbeidsplasser [Mobbing in worklife: A study on prevalence and health effects of mobbing in Norwegian workplaces].* Bergen: Forksningssenter for arbeidsmiljö (FAHS).

Frese, M. (1989). Gütekriterien der Operationalisierung von sozialer Unterstützung am Arbeitsplatz [Psychometric criteria of the operationalization of social support at work]. *Zeitschrift für Arbeitswissenschaft, 43*, 112–122.

Frese, M., & Zapf, D. (1987). Eine Skala zur Erfassung von Sozialen Stressoren am Arbeitsplatz [A scale measuring social stressors at work]. *Zeitschrift für Arbeitswissenschaft, 41*, 134–141.

Goffmann, E. (1967). *Stigma: über Techniken der Bewältigung beschädigter Identität [Stigma: On techniques of coping with damaged identity].* Frankfurt: Suhrkamp.

Groeblinghoff, D. (1994). Kostenaspekte bei nicht mobbingspezifischen Therapieansätzen [Aspects of costs of non mobbing-specific therapy approaches]. In M. Becker & D. Groeblinghoff (Eds.), *Therapiekonzeption der Brandenburgischen Klinik für Psychosomatik.* Neubrück bei Berlin: Brandenburgische Klinik für Psychosomatik.

Groeblinghoff, D. (1995). Folgen—Was kann Mobbing kosten [Consequences—what are the costs of mobbing]. In Landesbildungswerk der DAG Berlin und Brandenburg e.V. (Ed.), *Mobbing—Psychoterror am Arbeitsplatz* (pp. 59–63). Berlin: MK-Druck.

Groeblinghoff, D. (in press). On diagnostics, therapy, and vocational rehabilitation of mobbing victims. *Proceedings of the First Congress of the World Council for Psychotherapy.* Vienna: World Council for Psychotherapy, International Congress Organization Service GmbH.

Groeblinghoff, D., & Becker, M. (1995, April). Rehabilitation of harassment victims. *Paper presented at the Seventh European Congress on Work and Organizational Psychology*, Györ, Hungary.

Halama, P., Möckel, U., & Gräntzdörffer, W. (1994). *Die Halama Mobbing Studie [The Halama mobbing study]*. Bad Lippspringe, Germany: GpSM.

Halama, P., Möckel, U., & Gräntzdörffer, W. (1995). *Schikane am Arbeitsplatz ("Mobbing")—Aktuelle Ergebnisse [Maltreatment at the workplace (mobbing)—current results]*. Bad Lippspringe, Germany: GpSM.

Hohmeier, J. (1975). Stigmatisierung als sozialer Definitionsprozeß [Stigmatization as a social definition process]. In M. Brusten & J. Hohmeier (Eds), *Stigmatisierung* (Vol. 1). Neuwied: Luchterhand.

Knorz, C., & Zapf, D. (1996). Mobbing—eine extreme Form sozialer Stressoren am Arbeitsplatz [Mobbing—an extreme form of social stressors at work]. *Zeitschrift für Arbeits- und Organisationspsychologie, 40*, 12–21.

Lazarus, R.S., & Folkman, S. (1984). *Stress, appraisal, and coping*. New York: Springer.

Leymann, H. (1987). Självmord till följd av psykiskt våld i arbetslivet (Suicide as a consequence of psychological violence in work life]. In *Arbete, människa, miljö, 3*, 155–160.

Leymann, H. (1990). *Presentation av LIPT-formuläret. Konstruktion, validering, utfall [Presentation of the LIPT questionnaire: Construction, validation, outcome]*. Stockholm: Violen inom Praktikertjänst.

Leymann, H. (1993). *Mobbing. Psychoterror am Arbeitsplatz und wie man sich dagegen wehren kann [Mobbing—psychoterror at the workplace, and how one can defend oneself]*. Reinbek bei Hamburg: Rowohlt.

Leymann, H. (Ed.). (1995). *Der neue Mobbing Bericht—Erfahrungen und Initiativen, Auswege und Hilfsangebote [The new mobbing report—experiences and initiatives, ways out and help offers]*. Reinbek bei Hamburg: Rowohlt.

Leymann, H., & Gustafsson, A. (this issue). Mobbing and the development of post-traumatic stress disorders. *European Journal of Work and Organizational Psychology, 5*(2).

Leymann, H., & Gustavsson, B. (1984). *Psykiskt väld i arbetslivet. Två explorativa undersökningar [Psychological violence in workplaces. Two explorative studies]*. (Undersökningsrapport 42.) Stockholm: Arbetsskyddsstyrelsen.

Ludewig, K. (1992). *Systemische Therapie—Grundlagen klinischer Theorie und Praxis [Systematic therapy—basics of clinical theory and practice]*. Stuttgart: Klett-Cotta.

Niedl, K. (1995). *Mobbing/Bullying am Arbeitsplatz [Mobbing/bullying at the workplace]*. München und Mering: Rainer Hampp.

Paanen, T., & Vartia, M. (1991). *Mobbing at workplaces in state government*. Helsinki: Finnish Work Environment Fund.

Resch, M. (1994). *Wenn Arbeit krank macht [When work makes ill]*. Berlin: Ullstein.

Resch, M. (1995). Streßausgleich bei Mobbing—Einige Grundregeln [Coping with stress caused by mobbing—some basic rules]. In H. Leymann (Ed.), *Der neue Mobbing Bericht— Erfahrungen und Initiativen Auswege und Hilfsangebote [The new mobbing report— experiences and initiatives, ways out and help offers]*. Reinbek bei Hamburg: Rowohlt.

Semmer, N.K., & Dunckel, H. (1991). Streßbezogene Arbeitsanalyse [Stress oriented job analysis]. In S. Greif, E. Bamberg, & N.K. Semmer (Eds.), *Psychischer Streß am Arbeitsplatz* (pp. 57–90). Göttingen: Hogrefe.

Semmer, N.K., Zapf, D., & Dunckel, H. (1995). Assessing stress at work: A framework and an instrument. In O. Svane & C. Johansen (Eds.), *Work and health—scientific basis of progress in the working environment* (pp. 105–113). Luxembourg: Office for Official Publications of the European Communities.

Stierlin, H. (1975). *Von der Psychoanalyse zur Familientherapie [From psychoanalysis to family therapy]*. Stuttgart: Klett-Cotta.

World Health Organization. (1992). *International classification of diseases* (10th ed.) (ICD-10). Göttingen: Huber.

Zapf, D. (1993). Stress oriented job analysis of computerized office work. *The European Work and Organizational Psychologist, 3*(2), 85–100.

Zerssen, D.v. (1971). Die Beschwerden-Liste als Test [The complaint list as test]. *Therapiewoche 21*, 1908–1914. Karlsruhe: Braun.

EUROPEAN JOURNAL OF WORK AND ORGANIZATIONAL PSYCHOLOGY, 1996, 5 (2), 295–307

Mobbing—Prevention and Management in Organizations

Martin Resch

*Institut für Arbeitspsychologie und Arbeitspädagogik IAP,
Seevetal, Germany*

Marion Schubinski

Universität Konstanz, Germany

So far, only a few companies have dealt with the issue of "mobbing". This article describes some of the variables required for a successful implementation of an anti-mobbing programme, as well as measures of prevention and intervention. A successful anti-mobbing programme depends on the pressure the problem exerts on the company, the competition with other company programmes, the negative image of mobbing, and the slow diffusion of social issues in companies. Various prevention measures are outlined and suggested in connection with the causes of mobbing: changes in work design, changes in leadership behaviour, the protection of the individual social position, and the moral standard of employees. Depending on the stage of conflict escalation, different intervention measures apply. The concepts of appointing contact people for mobbing victims and the setting up of neutral clearing posts are discussed.

INTRODUCTION

Prevention programmes against mobbing in organizations, as with all company social programmes, can only be understood by looking at the complex structure of the various interest groups. Here, economics are rarely persuasive; even if an economist demonstrates that the resulting costs of mobbing are higher than the costs of the prevention, companies do not necessarily initiate anti-mobbing programmes (Niedl, 1995a, 1995b). Companies are more likely to invest in social programmes, to enhance their image both inside and outside the company, where the economic considerations are only marginal.

Requests for reprints should be addressed to M. Schubinski, Universität Konstanz, Fachgruppe Psychologie, Postfach 5560, D42, D-78434 Konstanz, Germany. Email: marion.schubinski@uni-konstanz.de

---

In the German-speaking countries, mobbing has been a public issue since 1992 (Leymann, 1995b). The media, the rapidly growing number of self-help groups for mobbing victims, and organizations such as trade unions and churches have all called for intervention and prevention measures such as anti-mobbing programmes in companies. Several measures have now been developed, but no systematic evaluation of such measures has so far taken place. The measures described in this article are based on case studies and personal experience.

In order to estimate the chances and the success of anti-mobbing programmes in companies, different variables require consideration. These variables, which are described below, through their interdependence can in turn affect the politics of a company.

Pressure of the Problem on the Company

Whenever a problem exerts strong pressure in the company, social programmes are often initiated. A parallel example is the establishment of alcohol prevention programmes. Very often it takes a spectacular case to motivate the company to deal with a known but unacknowledged problem. Only if a worker dies from the consequences of alcohol abuse or a fatal accident happens does the company agree to confront the problem (Fuchs, 1992). Newspapers reported that after the oil spill of the *Exxon Valdez*, where the captain was drunk, almost all large mineral oil companies started to run alcohol prevention programmes.

Regarding the mobbing issue, what different kinds of pressure exist in the company? The mobbing issue is being publicized by researchers, victims, the media, and psychological and management consultants. Unfortunately, of these parties, only the victims themselves are part of the organizational structure of the company and a feature of the mobbing process is that either the victims are isolated in the company or have already been fired (Leymann, 1993). So, what motivation is there for companies to confront this problem? At the moment, we know of only two pressure points that can make mobbing important to companies: on the one hand is public opinion against the company after mobbing cases become public; on the other hand is the pressure of the social service agency or the trade union representatives. As described later, at the moment it is mainly the social service agency and the union representatives that exert sufficient pressure on some companies.

Competition with Other Company Programmes

Those that take up the issue of mobbing in their company and start to plan a mobbing programme are in competition with many other managerial programmes (Neuberger, 1995): management programmes, conflict management training, alcohol prevention programmes, teambuilding programmes, employee grievance systems, employee suggestion schemes, etc. What value does a specific mobbing prevention programme have, especially since, as described later, preventive measures *per se* do not seem to be especially effective against mobbing? Instead, the mobbing programmes usually aim at improving the general organizational climate. For these reasons, many firms reject anti-mobbing programmes, stating that they already do what they can to prevent mobbing.

The Negative Image of the Mobbing Issue

The term "mobbing" has a very negative connotation: The association with the "mob" suggests the condemnation of an adversary as a heartless, cruel perpetrator. So companies dislike being associated with the term "mobbing". Compared to other programmes on well-being or affirmative action, the anti-mobbing programmes cannot be as easily used to improve the image of the firm. As with the issue of "alcohol on the job", many companies prefer the strategy of denying the existence of a problem for as long as possible.

Slow Diffusion of Social Issues in Companies

Social topics, discussed by the public, do have an impact on companies but with a long time delay. This may be exemplified by the establishment of alcohol prevention programmes. Fuchs (1992) subdivided the construction of company alcohol prevention programmes into four stages: (1) sensibility and testing of new measures, (2) transfer and generalization, (3) consolidation, and (4) critical review and revision.

According to Fuchs, the first stage began in the mid-1970s and the fourth stage was reached at the end of the 1980s. Hence, it took 15 years from the first public pressure and design of project models to establish alcohol prevention programmes in more than 2000 companies. Assuming that the same time frame is required for the mobbing issue, it is not surprising that acceptable prevention programmes have rarely been implemented. In the German public the onset of discussion began in the summer of 1992, since when only a few of the first initiatives have been undertaken by companies. Therefore, at the moment we are clearly only in the first stage of the process. It is still an open question whether the topic of mobbing will find wide acceptance in companies or if it will be subsumed in the general discussion about organizational well-being.

CATEGORIES OF PREVENTION MEASURES

The advice given in popular publications (e.g. Diergarten, 1994; Huber, 1993; Waniorek & Waniorek, 1994; Zuschlag, 1994) is rather ad hoc. The impression is given that there are anti-mobbing methods that work in any situation. Other authors refer to conflict escalation models (e.g. Resch, 1994; Walter, 1993), the most widely developed of which is the one by Glasl (1994). Glasl makes no reference to the mobbing process, although his classification embodies conflicts of this type. The underlying scheme of the various models is, depending on the development of the conflict, that different types of measures against mobbing are effective. Resch (1994) differentiates between: (1) prevention, (2) intervention in early stages, (3) intervention in the middle stages, and (4) support in the late stages. Prevention refers only to those measures that can be applied before any sign of a mobbing process is detectable, i.e. those that aim at the avoidance of mobbing before it becomes an issue.

There are three phases in the mobbing process (e.g. Leymann, 1993). One may speak of the *early phase* when the underlying conflict is still recognizable and all the participants can perceive the disputes and quarrels between people. This means, in general, that there exists a conflicting party A, a conflicting party B, and a neutral group.

In the *middle stage*, the participants no longer perceive a conflict between people, but rather between "us and the person". The original conflict has been pushed into the background. The rejection pertains not only to certain specific acts or behaviours, but rather towards the whole person. By now, the focus of attention is a certain person that "does not fit in". Although the conflict is still kept in the group or the department, the specific feature of this situation is that no neutral person is in the group. A polarization has taken place and now group pressure exists to make a decision.

The mobbing process enters its *late stage*, when group or department borders are crossed and official measures are implemented. These can be, for example, legal measures such as warnings, or transfers. In other cases, public remarks about the troublemaker or spreading rumours beyond the group are sufficient.

One has to differentiate company-oriented prevention and intervention measures from the individual measures of therapy, rehabilitation, and resocialization of victims. It is desirable that the measures of rehabilitation are followed through in alliance with the company. According to our knowledge, the legal situation allows this only in Sweden (Leymann, 1993). (Corresponding legal preconditions in other countries are unknown to us.)

In the case of already existing or developing mobbing conflicts, Neuberger (1995) considers of primary importance the distinction between preventive measures and effective intervention measures. In the following section, the distinction between prevention and intervention will be made. Our emphasis in this article is the perspective of companies and the measures they can initiate against mobbing. Individual measures, such as therapy and rehabilitation will therefore not be discussed here (see Groeblinghoff & Becker, this issue; Leymann & Gustafsson, this issue).

THE PREVENTION OF MOBBING

The causes of mobbing have not yet been sufficiently studied. Leymann (1993), based on several hundred case studies, assumes that four factors seem to be involved: (1) deficiencies in the work design, (2) deficiencies in leadership behaviour, (3) a socially exposed position of the victims, and (4) a low moral standard in the department. This coincides with the results of our own case studies and there is also some empirical evidence of the role of organizational factors such as work design and leadership behaviour (Einarsen, Raknes, & Matthiesen, 1994; Vartia, this issue; Zapf, Knorz, & Kulla, this issue).

Prevention measures may apply to all four causes. According to our experience in working with companies, there are however extreme inter-dependencies between different areas and levels in an organization. Changes in one area may very quickly lead to changes in other areas. All of these measures will most likely be ineffective if managers, for example, do not agree to change their behaviour (Volk, 1995). In addition, it is common knowledge in the organizational development business that organizational development measures will only be effective if supported by the top management (e.g. Neuberger, 1991). Nevertheless, the four potential causes provide a good classification and basis for possible prevention measures.

Changes in Work Design

Based on our experience, a change in work design often assists the early stages of the prevention of the mobbing. Well-designed jobs with low strain, high job control, and decision latitude reduce the possibility of letting built-up stress out on a scapegoat. Zapf et al. (this issue) found, for example, that time autonomy was significantly lower for mobbing victims than for a comparable group of office employees. Because conflict management needs time, little time autonomy may restrict the possibilities to solve conflicts when they first arise. (These are, of course, first results based on a small sample size which require confirmation in extended samples.)

In addition to the measures for direct improvement of work conditions, all measures that increase the control of the workers on the design of their work are suitable as prevention measures for the mobbing process. Different tested managerial models exist, for example project groups, employee suggestion systems, or employee programmes for well-being, and health circles (e.g. Breisig, 1990; Bundeszentrale für gesundheitliche Aufklärung, 1992). Project groups, employee programmes on well-being, and other discussion and participation models create collective options for change. This means that a group of employees can influence the design of their work conditions. A theoretical assumption is that stressors and strain produced by poor work conditions such as monotony, low decision latitude (Karasek & Theorell, 1990), role conflict and role ambiguity (Rizzo, House, & Lirtzman, 1970), and other organizational factors lead to interpersonal conflicts. Support for this argument can be drawn from a study by Marcelissen, Winnubst, Buunck, & DeWolff (1988) who found that stressors and strain produced by poor work conditions reduced the social support of co-workers. By measures such as health circles, project groups, and other participation models, workers take part in the process of work design. By improving the work conditions, strain is reduced with less chances for interpersonal conflicts. Thereby, frustration with poor work design is reduced, giving less need to take things out on a scapegoat.

Changes in Leadership Behaviour

Additional prevention methods must apply to leadership behaviour. In management training, this incorporates the skill to recognize conflicts and to handle them productively. At the same time, warning signals of the beginning mobbing process need to be recognized. For the prevention of mobbing, it probably would be sufficient if the concepts taught in modern management are actually realized in leadership behaviour. Unfortunately, as experience shows, leadership principles, as good as they sound, are often not taken seriously (Neuberger & Kompa, 1993; Volk, 1995).

In order to change the leadership culture of the company it is not enough to provide training for middle management. A change is more likely, for example if:

1. The new leadership style is practised first by top management. By taking a top-down approach, top management serves as a role model. Values set by top management are more easily integrated in the corporate culture (e.g. Sackmann, 1983). Through mentoring or coaching, the leadership style may be passed on to the other levels of the hierarchy.

2. The new leadership styles are learned on the job, in real situations, instead of just being rehearsed in workshops outside the organization. The transfer of learned material is increased if stimulus and response elements in the learning situation indicate high similarity to the real work situation (Baldwin & Ford, 1988). Therefore, learning on the job reduces the difficulty of transferring the new skills to the job. Concepts such as supervision and coaching resemble techniques of on-the-job training skills.

3. The result of the management training is evaluated, e.g. through regular appraisals by the employees. The successful acquisition of new skills is dependent on the quality of the training. In that sense, an evaluation serves as an important feedback tool for determining the quality of the

training (e.g. Nork, 1989). Through regular appraisals by employees, deficits and problems concerning the training may be detected.

Improvement in the Social Position of Each Individual

In addition to the possibility of designing collective work conditions, grievance rules must be implemented that protect the individual, even if he or she opposes the general viewpoint of a group. This kind of influence is especially difficult to establish—on the other hand, only a functioning grievance system and conflict model can prevent an individual from becoming a mobbing victim because of his/her socially exposed position.

Although individual grievance rights are planned to be incorporated in the "Betriebsverfassungsgesetz" (German regulations governing industrial relations), this right is almost never practised, because the victims are afraid of sanctions. Therefore, this formal law must be supplemented through a company-accepted grievance procedure which should include aspects such as anonymity, clear rules, experts on how grievance systems work, people who can be asked for advice, etc.

There exist different kinds of grievance and conflict models (Breisig, 1990; Glasl, 1994). The most cautious kind of conflict model is the moderating procedure. A conflict model may declare that each conflict party has the right to ask for a talk with the opponent under the supervision of a neutral moderator (Sheppard, 1983). If this does not work, negotiations can be implemented. Here, a mediator from the outside can be employed, making a mediating suggestion to each party. These negotiations must proceed according to fixed rules (e.g. the same amount of time for each party to present their views and make suggestions for negotiation, the right for time out, and the right to reject the suggestion). Whenever the negotiations that are working towards an agreement fail, a solution is decided by a referee. Unlike the negotiation process, the decision of an impartial referee need not be accepted by both sides (Sheppard, 1983).

By comparing the tasks and goals of the mediator and the referee, the mediator controls the interaction between the parties, but allows them to make their own decision (Sheppard, 1983). The referee enters the process whenever the two parties have not found an agreement. He or she listens passively to the disputing parties' arguments and then gives a decision.

Company conflict models must be discussed more widely and written down afterwards, for example as company and work agreements. A commitment to recognize such a conflict model in a special section of the work contract is also a possibility. Written regulations on conflict management gain more acceptance and also raise awareness that the company is actually taking measures.

Raising Moral Standards in the Department

Leymann (1993) believes that most mobbing processes can be prevented from the start by committed superiors or even by courageous co-workers. According to his experience, in order to proceed against mobbing there must be a mutual understanding of what behaviour of co-workers is acceptable and what is unfair. As with Kohlberg's theory on the development of moral judgement (Lempert, 1988), Leymann proceeds from the basis of the influence of training programmes on the development of the "moral standard". A few companies have been willing to speak out officially against mobbing in their firm, e.g. in interviews or commentaries in company magazines.

Leymann had previously gained experience with constructing training material in Sweden. This material can be used to enable discussions with employees. Trained moderators instruct the work group. Generally, all workers of the company should participate in these groups. The group task lasts from about half to one day. The goal of the group task is a moral-ethical discussion with the workers about the causes and consequences of mobbing. The material from Leymann has been translated into German (Leymann, 1995a).

INTERVENTION OF THE MOBBING PROCESS

Even extremely cautious mobbing prevention cannot rule out the possibility that mobbing will evolve. To supplement prevention, measures need to be agreed upon that apply in the early, middle, and late phases of the mobbing conflict. The main suggestions are the naming of company contact people and the setting up of neutral clearing posts.

Contact People for Mobbing Victims

The system of contacts for mobbing victims, which can be implemented with relative little expenditure, is already practised in a number of companies, similarly to the principle of minority representatives (for disabled people, ethnic minorities, or women). This model should only be applied under three conditions:

1. The contact people must come from different departments, so that every mobbing victim can find a neutral contact person. If the contact person, for example, is on the work council, conflicts between co-workers cannot be revealed. Positive experience is gained whenever contact persons are drawn from employee representatives, from the personnel department, or from the social services.

2. The contact persons must be well trained for their task. This is frequently a problem. Mobbing is often apparent in the media and in popular

books, so many people consider themselves to be experts. Thus, the special features of mobbing compared to occasional harassment at the workplace, quarrels, or generally poor company climate often get lost. It is expected that a mobbing representative occupies himself/herself intensively with the mobbing issue and has attended specific training.

3. The opportunity must be given for contact people to talk about the problems and to propose solutions across the organizational hierarchy. As contact people, they should not only listen to the complaints of the victims but also prevent the escalation of mobbing.

Contact people can be overburdened with the resolution of very difficult cases of mobbing, since generally they do not possess the competence or status to make decisions. So it makes sense to supplement the system of contact people with a continuous or on-call "clearing post".

Impartial Clearing Posts

If the traditional company conflict strategies do not work because the opposition is too deeply involved in the conflict it may help to have the intervention of a neutral clearing post. It is important that the clearing posts are placed with competent people possessing psychological as well as legal knowledge. The tasks and competencies of the clearing post must be described specifically. This is usually done in company agreements. The strict neutrality of the clearing post against all company functions must be contained in the company agreement (Grund, 1995).

As an alternative to company clearing posts, external consultants could be employed to function as mediators. Leymann (1993) reports some cases in which he functioned as an external mediator. The disadvantage of this model is that it takes a special initiative to involve an external consultant. It is questionable whether a lowly employee is likely to have the courage to ask for an external consultant in order to resolve a conflict when his or her supervisor sits on the board of directors. External consultants often lack the specific insider knowledge that is required to understand a specific event. On the other hand, an external consultant is more likely to view a case from a less involved and in that sense more neutral perspective.

THE STATE OF REALIZATION

At the moment, mobbing is an issue of urgent concern. Niedl (1995b) lists only three firms that are confronting the topic directly. Likewise only a handful of specific companies are known to us that are actively dealing with the problem of mobbing. Of course, there may be considerably more organizations whose efforts in dealing with mobbing have not become public. The following refers to the activities in the public domain.

Most companies work on the topic internally. This can be measured to some extent by the increase of management training in 1994, for managers or for work councils and staff councils, that discuss the topic of mobbing. Another indicator may be given by the relatively large number of companies for which we performed training and management development covering the problems of mobbing.

We have surveyed 15 companies that offered training programmes on mobbing in 1993. Out of these 15 companies from completely different industries and of different sizes, seven had publicly discussed the topic of mobbing inside the company, through articles in company magazines or announcements by management. Those seven companies had also desig- nated mobbing contact persons, mostly in the area of social services. In one case, the works council or women representatives were also involved, in another case the company doctor, the personnel department, and the work council were added as contact places. In these companies the initiative came from the social agency (three out of seven) or from the company doctor (two out of seven). In one case the initiative came from the personnel department. In another case it came from the staff council. Two additional companies had not carried out any public activity, but had performed internal training with decision makers. In both cases the initiative came from the work council. Five of the surveyed companies did not see the necessity for action on the topic of mobbing.

Other studies, using similar surveys (Halama & Möckel, 1995; Horn, 1994; Nosthoff, 1993) report even less interest by companies in the topic. This difference is likely to have been a result of our study specifically addressing companies who had sent people to relevant training pro- grammes.

Various authors (e.g. Färber, Resch, & Werner, 1994; Grund, 1995) have suggested company agreements ("Betriebsvereinbarungen") against mobbing. Some authors raise some legitimate objections against a formal policy: Grund (1995) emphasizes that a company agreement cannot replace an intensive confrontation with mobbing; Neuberger (1995) fears that a formal regulation, in the case of actual conflict, can be used as means of putting pressure on the mobbing process. According to our experience it makes sense to first collect managerial experiences with different inter- vention strategies and then, after an intensive evaluation, to develop a written company regulation. Therefore, looking at the current experience companies have with mobbing, it would be too early to phrase explicit company regulations concerning mobbing. We are not aware of such company policies in Germany.

RESUMÉ

The concern of companies with the topic of mobbing is still in its early stages. Companies fear open discussion of the issue in their company, mainly because they are anxious about the company's image. Discussions within the company, worker education programmes, and specific management training exist in some companies, many have even designated contact persons. These activities tend to be called for and initiated by an isolated committed person, usually the company doctor or workers of the social agency, sometimes by the work council, or more rarely by the personnel department.

Given the various other problems companies face, only time will tell if mobbing will become an important item on the agenda. In the context of general management training programmes and general company programmes on well-being, there exists a strong tendency to drop the topic of mobbing. At the moment, next to the interests of management and psychology consultants, the victims themselves represent the strongest force to keep the mobbing issue alive. Their position and influence in the company, as a result of the mobbing process, is very much weakened, so that it is not likely that their viewpoint on the problem will be accepted by the company in the long run. In view of the high individual, company, and social costs of unrestrained mobbing processes, one can only appeal to the company decision makers to give this issue a great deal more attention.

REFERENCES

Baldwin, T.T., & Ford, J.K. (1988). Transfer of training: A review and directions for future research. *Personnel Psychology, 41*, 63–105.

Breisig, T. (1990). Betriebliche Sozialtechniken [Company social techniques]. *Handbuch für Betriebsrat und Personalwesen*. Neuwied: Luchterhand.

Bundeszentrale für gesundheitliche Aufklärung. (1992). *Gesundheitsförderung in der Arbeitswelt [Health promotion in working life]*. Köln: Author.

Diergarten, E. (1994). *Mobbing. Wenn der Arbeitsalltag zum Alptraum wird . . . [Mobbing: When the working day becomes a nightmare . . .]*. Köln: Bund-Verlag.

Einarsen, S., Raknes, B.I., & Matthiesen, S.B. (1994). Bullying and harassment at work and its relationship with work environment quality: An exploratory study. *The European Work and Organizational Psychologist, 4*(4), 381–401.

Färber, C., Resch, M., & Werner, H. (1994). *". . . noch nicht zu spät . . ." [". . . not yet too late . . ."]*. Hamburg: Kooperationsstelle Hamburg and IAP Institut für Arbeitspsychologie und Arbeitspädagogik e.V.

Fuchs, R. (1992). Sucht am Arbeitsplatz. Ein nicht mehr zu verleugnendes Thema [Addiction in the workplace: A theme that cannot be denied anymore]. *Sucht, 38*, 48–55.

Glasl, F. (1994). *Konfliktmanagement. Ein Handbuch für Führungskräfte und Berater [Conflict management: A handbook for managers and counsellors]* (4th ed.). Bern: Verlag Paul Haupt.

Grund, U. (1995). Wenn die Hemmschwellen sinken. Die Aufgabe der Gewerkschaft: Aufklärung und Prävention [When the threshold of scruples shrink: The task of the trade unions: Information and prevention]. In H. Leymann (Ed.), *Der neue Mobbing-Bericht. Erfahrungen und Initiativen, Aufwege und Hilfsangebote* (pp. 93–107). Reinbeck: Rowohlt.

Halama, P., & Möckel, U. (1995). "Mobbing". Acht Beiträge szum Thema Psychoterror am Arbeitsplatz ["Mobbing": Eight contributions to the subject of psychological terror at work]. In Evangelischer Pressedienst (Ed.), *epd-Dokumentation* (Vol. 11/95). Frankfurt a.M.: Gemeinschaftswerk der Evangelischen Publizistik.

Horn, A. (1994). *Ursachenanalyse, Kostenanalyse und Ansätze zur Problembewältigung von Mobbing in Großbetrieben [Cause analysis, cost analysis, and the approaches to cope with mobbing in big companies].* Unpublished diploma thesis. Stuttgart.

Huber, H. (1993). *Psychoterror am Arbeitsplatz. Mobbing [Psychoterror at work: Mobbing].* Niederhausen/Ts.: Falken-Verlag.

Karasek, R.A., & Theorell, T. (1990). *Healthy work: Stress, productivity, and the reconstruction of working life.* New York: Basic Books.

Lempert, W. (1988). *Moralisches Denken. Seine Entwicklung jenseits der Kindheit und seine Beeinflussung in der Sekundarstufe II [Moral thinking: Its development after childhood and influencing it in the secondary school].* Essen: Neue Deutsche Schule Verlagsgesellschaft.

Leymann, H. (1993). *Mobbing—Psychoterror am Arbeitsplatz und wie man sich dagegen wehren kann [Mobbing—psychoterror at work and how one can defend oneself].* Reinbeck: Rowohlt.

Leymann, H. (1995a). Begleitkoffer zum Buch Mobbing, Psychoterror am Arbeitsplatz. [Accompanying material to the book *Mobbing, psychoterror at work*]. Wien: Verlag des Österreichischen Gewerkschaftsbundes.

Leymann, H. (1995b). Einführung: Mobbing. Das Konzept und seine Resonanz in Deutschland [Introduction: Mobbing. The concept and its resonance in Germany]. In H. Leymann (Ed.), *Der neue Mobbingbericht. Erfahrungen und Initiativen, Auswege und Hilfsangebote* (pp. 13–26). Reinbeck: Rowohlt.

Marcelissen, F.H., Winnubst, J.A., Buunck, B., & DeWolff, C.J. (1988). Social support and occupational stress: A causal analysis. *Social Science and Medicine, 26,* 365–373.

Neuberger, O. (1991). *Personalentwicklung [Personnel development].* Stuttgart: Enke.

Neuberger, O. (1995). *Mobbing. Übel mitspielen in Organisationen [Mobbing—unfair play with people in organizations]* (2nd ed.). München: Rainer Hampp Verlag.

Neuberger, O., & Kompa, A. (1993). *Wir, die Firma. Der Kult um die Unternehmenskultur [We, the company. The idolization of organizational culture].* München: Heyne-Verlag.

Niedl, K. (1995a) *Mobbing/Bullying am Arbeitsplatz. Eine empirische Analyse zum Phänomen sowie zu personalwirtschaftlich relevanten Effekten von systematischen Feindseligkeiten [Mobbing/bullying at work: An empirical analysis of the phenomenon and of the effects of systematic hostilities relevant for human resource issues].* München: Rainer Hampp Verlag.

Niedl, K. (1995b). Wem nützt Mobbing? Psychoterror am Arbeitsplatz und die Personal wirtschaft von Unternehmen [For whom is mobbing useful? Psychoterror at work and personnel management of companies]. In H. Leymann (Ed.), *Der neue Mobbing-Bericht. Erfahrungen und Initiativen, Auswege und Hilfsangebote* (pp. 55–75). Reinbeck: Rohwohlt.

Nork, M. (1989). Management training: Evaluation, probleme, lösungsansätze. München: Rainer Hampp Verlag.

Nosthoff, M. (1993). *Das Phänomen Mobbing—eine neue Aufgabe betrieblicher Sozialarbeit [The phenomenon of mobbing—a new task for occupational social work].* Unpublished diploma thesis. Münster.

Resch, M. (1994). *Wenn Arbeit krank macht [When work makes ill].* Frankfurt a.M.: Ullstein-Verlag.

Rizzo, J.R., House, R.J., & Lirtzman, S.I. (1970). Role conflict and role ambiguity in complex organizations. *Administrative Science Quarterly, 15*, 150–163.

Sackmann, S. (1983). Organisationskultur: Die unsichtbare Einflußgröße [Organizational culture: The invisible impact factor]. *Gruppendynamik, 4*, 393–406.

Sheppard, B.H. (1983). Managers as inquisitors: Some lessons from the law. In M. Staw & L.L. Cummings (Eds.), *Negotiating in organizational behavior* (Vol. 6, pp. 193–213). Beverly Hills, CA: Sage.

Volk, H. (1995). Acht Thesen zu einer brisanten Entwicklung. Verhaltensverfall in den Unternehmen [Eight theses on an explosive development: Decay of behaviour in companies]. *Office-Management*, (5), 63.

Walter, H. (1993). *Mobbing: Kleinkrieg am Arbeitsplatz. Konflikte erkennen, offenlegen und lösen [Mobbing guerilla war at the workplace: Identifying, disclosing and solving conflicts]*. Frankfurt a.M.: Campus-Verlag.

Waniorek, L., & Waniorek, A. (1994). *Mobbing: Wenn der Arbeitsplatz zur Hölle wird [Mobbing. When the workplace becomes a hell]*. München: mvg-Verlag.

Zuschlag, B. (1994). *Mobbing—Schikane am Arbeitsplatz [Mobbing—harassment at work]*. Göttingen: Hogrefe-Verlag.

EUROPEAN JOURNAL OF WORK AND ORGANIZATIONAL PSYCHOLOGY, 1996, *5* (2) 309–320

PROFESSIONAL NEWS SECTION
John Toplis, Editor

CONTENTS

Copy and information for the Professional News Section should be sent to John Toplis, Management Development and Career Adviser, Training and Development Group, The Post Office, 49 Featherstone Street, London EC1Y 8SY. Telephone 0171-320 4214; Fax 0171-320 4216. The Section Editor's views are not necessarily those of the British Post Office.

INTRODUCTION TO THE PROFESSIONAL NEWS SECTION
John Toplis

The Professional News Section which follows is devoted to a single topic—a review of the Level 'A' Open Learning Programme published by the British Psychological Society.[1]

The programme was written by Professor David Bartram and Dr. Patricia Lindley and costs £165 (£150 to BPS members). The review is written by Dr. Jeannette James, a former colleague at The Post Office, who continues to work with us on an occasional basis.

I am publishing Dr. James's review for three reasons. First, it helps to clarify the current situation regarding the supply of tests in the UK.

---

[1]Available from the British Psychological Society, St. Andrew's House, 48 Princess Road East, Leicester, LE1 7DR, UK.

In terms of making tests available to non-psychologists I believe that the British approach is broadly in line with the United States and Australia, but that it contrasts with much of Europe where reputable tests are supplied only to fully qualified psychologists.

Second, the review should help readers assess the learning materials and whether they might be used in other training situations. Third, I would like to encourage debate in the Professional Newsletter about the relative merits and disadvantages of the contrasting approaches to the establishment and maintenance of test standards adopted by Britain and its national partners within the EC.

Some Background Information

Major UK Test Publishers supply their tests to both psychologists and non-psychologists. However, there are differences in the amount of training considered appropriate for the two groups.

For many years, the British Psychological Society (BPS) sought to encourage good training by approving every training course, and considerable detail had to be supplied to the BPS Steering Committee on Test Standards. This included information about the psychologist responsible for running the course, the test in which training was to be given, and a detailed timetable for the course.

In time, at least three disadvantages became apparent. First, as the use of tests and the numbers of courses increased, the workload for the committee (comprising psychologists working on a voluntary and unpaid basis) increased dramatically. Second, those seeking training in a further test from a different supplier often had to repeat much of the introductory and background training. Third, there was no way of making training available to those test users who were not dealing with the major test suppliers; without such information, these test users were unlikely to recognize the shortcomings in tests that they were using.

In the light of this experience the BPS felt that a certification scheme in the use of tests in occupational settings was required. The review that follows is about distance learning material designed to help those who study it to reach Level A. Level A covers the competencies needed to evaluate, administer, and interpret most group-administered ability and aptitude tests, interest inventories, and careers guidance materials.

It should be stressed that study of the material does not automatically lead to the award of a Level A certificate; rather an individual has to demonstrate their comptetence to a Chartered Psychologist whose name appears on a special register approved and maintained by the British Psychological Society.

PSYCHOLOGICAL TESTING: REVIEW OF THE LEVEL 'A' OPEN LEARNING PROGRAMME

Jeannette James

Introduction

The main aims of the Open Learning Programme are to provide an alternative, more flexible, and cheaper method of acquiring Level A training, i.e. a distance learning package, and to provide useful resource materials to providers of courses.

It comprises seven distance learning modules, three of them in two parts; an introduction and study guide, including a section of basic mathematical procedures and a glossary of terms; a test pack for practical work including copies of a specially made test for practice use, administration instructions, conversion tables, candidate evaluation forms, etc.; and an Assessment Portfolio intended as a record of performance on the various tasks set. The latter is particularly useful in that it reproduces all the questions and exercises from the modules, with space for answers and notes, in one separate book. It is also necessary to have access to major publishers' catalogues and the BPS *Review of Psychometric Tests for Assessment in Vocational Training.* (Bartram et al., 1990).

The seven modules are: (1) Psychological Testing: an Introduction (2) Scaling, Norms, and Standardization (2 parts) (3) Reliability and the Standard Error of Measurement (2 parts) (4) Validity and Fairness in Testing (2 parts) (5) Test Administration and Scoring (6) Test Interpretation (7) Choosing Tests.

Review

The pack of materials is well presented and relatively easy to find one's way around. The coverage (largely dictated by the Level A competences, which were decided by a BPS working party, see Appendix A) is wide, and many complex and difficult to explain issues are put across very well. There are a large, but not excessive, number of questions and exercises as one works through the texts. Herein lies a possible problem for assessors: They will have to check understanding (to some extent) independently of the Assessment Portfolio as clear and thorough answers are normally provided by the authors. However, this is not an insurmountable problem, and should certainly not be regarded as a reason for providing less satisfactory answers. The questions and exercises are generally well chosen, involving real thought and not just regurgitation of the text. The 'thinking questions' and the practical exercises, e.g. some excellent self-assessment questions on norms in Module 6, merit particular mention. Graphical and diagrammatic representations are generally used where possible to help clarify the text. These will help many students, but there may be others who find them confusing or puzzling, and who may understand better from the written text alone.

311

It is usually advisable to warn students that this is a very individual matter, and to explain that sometimes explanations are, in effect, given twice; once purely verbally and once with say, graphs plus some words. In some cases, of course, graphs or diagrams are virtually essential. Nonetheless, the non-diagram minded student needs to be borne in mind; they can actually find such representations difficult, or even confusing, rather than clarifying. However, there are some very good illustrative tables, including an interesting example explained in the text, of the problems of interpreting ipsative scores.

It is not altogether clear why the coverage of some issues, e.g. the relationship between validity and reliability, needs to be so detailed and/or theoretical (at Level A). It would be understandable if the competences specified this, but occasionally the coverage seems to go well beyond that required by the competences, e.g. standard error of measurement. Many students are likely, therefore, to need varying degrees of assistance with some parts of the Level A pack, particularly if they are not psychologists and/or find numerical material difficult. Fortunately the authors do warn readers about the considerable extra time they may have to spend on the difficult Modules 2 and 3. As these provide the main technical background to test use, and each consists of 2 parts, they do, in fact, constitute the major part of the Learning Programme in terms of length, and definitely the major part in terms of time. However, it should be noted that the material is only occasionally highly numerical, and that it is not possible to explain the use of, say, the standard error of measurement, without making use of numbers.

Another example of possibly giving too much detail is the discussion of validity generalization. The explanation is excellent and very thorough, illustrating why the topic is important both practically and theoretically, discussing situational specificity, explaining how to combine results from several validity studies (as might be provided in a manual), using weighted (by sample size) averages, and describing the drawbacks and problems. This would be useful to most occupational psychologists, let alone the wider range of people who will be studying for Level A competence; it certainly goes beyond describing the basic notions and yet, arguably, the Level A competences do not require this. Use of 'optional boxes', as provided at certain other points in the text, might be a possible solution here, and in similar circumstances elsewhere.

It is also debatable as to whether it is vital (not optional) for students to know how to calculate certain statistics themselves, e.g. correlations. Doing it oneself is undoubtedly one of the best ways to learn statistics, but performing complex calculations may distract students from the more important matter of understanding what a statistic is, and how to use and interpret it. In certain sections there is a great deal of computation, some of which is not essential given the clear text explanations: This risks deterring some students who may skip sections or worry unduly about understanding the mathematics.

Overall, although excellent on theory, the Programme is weak on the practical issues of choosing (or not) tests and dealing with clients when, as is most often the case, they are not the actual people taking the tests. As these matters are important for most practitioners, it is somewhat worrying that this weakness reflects their low profile in the Level A competences (see Appendix A). However, there is scope for interpretation and, as has been noted earlier, in many instances the interpretation put upon the competences in this Programme has resulted in a tendency to include more than is essentially required; yet the texts oversimplify the practical issues, underplay the 'real life' problems, and do not take a sufficiently pragmatic approach.

Full answers to the exercises involving choosing possible tests from catalogues and evaluating cost effectiveness are not given, no doubt because it is desirable for students to use real catalogues for such exercises (and these change from year to year). Fortunately, as it allows proper answers to be provided by the authors, the other exercises involve evaluations using the *BPS Review of Psychometric Tests for Assessment in Vocational Training* (Bartram et al., 1990). It is, however understandable in the circumstances, a great pity that so little attention is given to examples of cases where tests may *not* be appropriate.

Whilst it is fitting for such a Programme to present ideals to aim for, it does not explain that these are seldom fully attainable in practice; readers need guidance in which aspects can be allowed to 'slip', and which cannot, e.g. it is essential to use reliable instruments suitable for the level and type of job. Test users seeking information from publishers, as recommended, on, for example, ethnic differences, are likely to be disappointed. In most cases the data do not appear to exist, at least for suitable or large enough samples, and publishers often seem reluctant to publish them even when they do. The 'ideal' response to this is to try to identify a suitable test by trialling several, performing a validity study and checking on ethnic differences in test scores and differential validity. This is seldom possible, even for those of us with the relevant expertise, as clients are reluctant to fund such studies and wait for the results. It is far more common in practice to make a choice as best one can from among the suitable tests available, using limited and often unsatisfactory information; the test will frequently go straight into use with, one hopes, careful monitoring and, in due course, a validity study. The problem of ethnic differences is hugely complicated by the fact that this area is a minefield, even for the wary, and will improve only when publishers take a greater responsibility for it (as some are beginning to do). It is exacerbated by the low sample sizes for certain ethnic groups among job applicants/holders, to say nothing of the differential performance of different ethnic groups and the regional nature of the differences.

Given their importance, it is surprising that clients are scarcely mentioned in the Programme, except in connection with interpreting tests appropriately for them. In practice, dealing with the clients can be

313

difficult, whether one is internal or external to the organization, a psychologist or a personnel practitioner. In the commonest situation, that of a personnel practitioner using tests within his or her own organization, the internal clients are often more senior. Whilst they may not argue with internal lawyers or medical officers, most do not recognize personnel staff as experts in this sense (perhaps correctly, as personnel staff are frequently unqualified); the sorts of assessments used are often arrived at by way of negotiation of some kind between such a client and the personnel practitioner. Occupational psychologists have greater acceptance as 'experts', but can still suffer from their position in the organization and the need to retain clients' goodwill (be they internal or external).

Ideally, the learning pack should provide Level A students with arguments to to use when they are being pressed, for instance, to use a test which they know to be unsuitable. In fact, most of the relevant points are covered somewhere in the Programme, but it does not bring them together or raise the issue of dealing with clients. This reflects a similar weakness in the Level A competences which is unfortunate, given, for example, that clients sometimes have to be warned of the possible risk of an industrial tribunal if they persist in certain courses of action. In fact some of us feel that more complaints and tribunals might not be a bad thing, since they would improve personnel practice in the UK.

Module 6 rightly highlights standards of feedback and confidentiality but, again, does not reflect the practical problems likely to be encountered in, for instance, giving full feedback to everyone tested. This is costly, and can actually be almost impossible in the time available, even if the client is committed to giving feedback (which they may not be, particularly for external candidates). A compromise can usually be reached but, once again, the Programme could give a more realistic picture of the likely issues and difficulties. there is a danger that practitioners, finding they cannot achieve the ideal presented, will abandon altogether, say, feedback to external candidates, dismissing what they have read as totally impractical in the real world of clients and time pressures.

The programme is also decidedly weak on the costs and benefits of using tests, devoting only half a page or so directly to the issue. Again, this reflects the lack of attention given to this subject in the Level A competences. Nonetheless, as noted earlier, these are open to interpretation; the one relating to benefits and losses rightly does not restrict itself to the financial sphere, and issues of test acceptability, administrative practicality, etc. are briefly dealt with in the pack. However, the financial aspects are scarcely mentioned at all. Considering the space devoted to some of the other topics mentioned earlier, this seems a serious omission. How are practitioners to know, and be able to communicate to their clients, what the (cost) benefits are of using tests?

It is possible to impart the basic principles of utility analysis (a method of calculating the cost benefits of using tests of certain validity with certain numbers of staff, etc.) fairly easily (see Smith, 1988). Whilst the detailed calculations can become highly complex if one wishes to take into account such factors as opportunity costs, inflation, staff retention time, etc., it is, in most cases, not essential to do this; the likely saving achieved by using a particular test in a particular context can be calculated quite easily making conservative assumptions. Whilst the formula is simple enough, there are some practical problems associated with it, e.g. assigning a value to good staff as opposed to poor ones. This Learning Programme is not the place to go into these sorts of details. However, it would be appropriate to explain the basic principles of utility analysis or, at the very least, to describe simple ways in which likely cost benefits can be estimated. A further advantage of this is that it would highlight the importance of validity.

There are a few other points of concern, some regarding issues which are inherently difficult, or present particular problems in presentation to a lay audience (and on which not all psychologists agree). Three different examples will be mentioned here. First, in view of the tendency of most people to value quantity over quality in samples, Module 2 tends to overemphasize size at the expense of representativeness, at least in Part 1. However, in fairness, Part 2, whilst still tending to underplay specific norms (as opposed to general ones), does encourage the use of local norms where appropriate, and provides a good practical example.

Second, having given a very thorough explanation of confidence intervals, including asymmetric true score confidence limits and regression to the menu (*not* optional), the relevant section concludes with a 'rule of thumb' using reliability estimates. This seems a sharp and possibly dangerous shift from (perhaps) over-sophisticated to over-simplification. Third, like most discussions of fairness in testing, Module 4 seems to draw heavily in the USA. This is understandable but unfortunate: it is UK and EC law that applies in the UK.

In spite of these criticisms, this pack is an impressive and extremely useful set of open learning materials. The reviewer has some 17 years experience of teaching research methodology in the social sciences for the Open University at both undergraduate and postgraduate levels; this involves assisting and assessing students who do almost all their studying with distance learning materials. Some of the ground covered is the same as, or similar to, certain parts of Level A, e.g. reliability and validity. Many students, even those following a psychology degree course, had difficulty with some of the concepts involved, and with anything numerical or graphical; it seems probable, therefore, that Level A Programme students will have similar problems.

Some of them will be psychologists as, in the UK, psychology degrees (even postgraduate occupational psychology degrees) do not cover enough psychometrics to make graduates automatically eligible for Level A competence certificates. However, psychologists should find the ideas and concepts involved much more accessible than non-psychologists. It may be, for instance, that most psychologists could study the Open Learning Programme alone, complete the Assessment Portfolio provided, register and then, without attending any formal course, satisfy an assessor of their competence in the various areas. However, it seems likely that the pack will be used most often in conjunction with other methods of learning; this does not in any way detract from its general usefulness but it does mean that students using it alone may encounter difficulties. A demand for very short courses covering the more complex issues may arise.

It is also probable that, in the future, combinations of distance/open learning and attendance at courses will become more common. This may well be a more effective way of taking in some quite complex material than intensive full time courses particularly as the starting points of learners are likely to be very varied.

In addition, it is likely that the materials will be useful as revision and resource materials for those who do not use tests continually, and who may need reference materials to remind them of key points. The overviews, aims, and summaries provided in each module will be particularly helpful in this respect.

However, despite the thorough and often impressive explanations, some students are likely to have difficulty in understanding certain concepts and issues. It is heartening to see some important and commonly misunderstood points made very clearly, e.g. that validity is relative and not absolute, and that no instrument is valid in a vacuum but can only be called valid in particular contexts.

The programme's weaknesses partly reflect those of the Level A competences, but its excellent explanations and coverage of some complex issues are likely to be infinitely better than the vast majority of Level A courses. It would make useful reading for all users of psychometric tests, whether they are already trained to Level A or not.

REFERENCES

Bartram, D. et al. (1990 but updates available). *Review of psychometric tests for assessment in vocational training.* Leicester, UK: BPS Books.

Smith, M. (1988). Calculating the sterling value of selection. *Guidance and Assessment Review, 4*(1), 6–8. Leicester, UK: BPS.

APPENDIX A

SUMMARY OF BRITISH PSYCHOLOGICAL SOCIETY LEVEL A UNITS OF COMPETENCE

NB The seven modules in the Level A pack do not follow exactly the seven units outlined here, i.e. issues are covered in a different order, etc. This is for the practical reasons of effective teaching and dealing with issues in a logical order for students.

Unit 1 Psychology Testing: Defining Assessment Needs

This unit deals with the general categorization of types of assessment instrument and covers some underlying psychological theory and background to ability testing, e.g. general and specific abilities, influence of environmental factors. Job and task analysis are covered in so far as they relate to assessment; competence in job analysis is not assumed but ability to evaluate critically the results of job analyses is.

Unit 2 Basic Principles of Scaling and Standardization

This deals with the fundamental statistical concepts required to use psychological tests. Most undergraduate psychology courses in the UK cover this material, as do some other social science courses, e.g. means, standard deviations, frequency distributions, sample size and standard error of the mean, confidence limits, percentiles, raw and standardized scores (Z-scores, T-scores, Stens, Stanines), using norms and conversion tables, ipsative and non-ipsative scales.

Unit 3 The Importance of Reliability and Validity

This unit gives thorough coverage of the issues including: interpreting correlations obtained under different conditions; the basic premises of classical test theory ('true scores' and random error); pros and cons of different methods of estimating reliability; sources of error; effect of test length; range restriction and adjustments; standard error of measurement and how to use it; standard errors of difference between, and sum of, two scale scores; basic Generalizability Theory; types of validity and the relationship between reliability and validity; the extent to which one can generalize; pros and cons of different methods of assessing concurrent and predictive validity and the effects of selection on the latter.

Unit 4 Deciding when Psychological Tests should or should not be used as part of an Assessment Process

This unit covers a range of issues, some of which are expanded on in other units, e.g. the law relating to sex and ethnic discrimination; identifying suitable tests from catalogues and then, from the manuals, appropriate information regarding matters such as rationale, reliability, validity, norms, administration requirements and any restrictions on use; judging which test (if any) is most suitable and which norms; deciding how best to use the test(s) to maximize usefulness and minimize risks.

Unit 5 *Administering Tests to one or more Candidates and dealing with Scoring Procedures*

This is a very practical skill-based unit emphasizing good professional practices in test administration, ensuring standard conditions and fairness. It includes practical planning and preparation, appropriate locations and advance information to candidates, security and confidentiality, different scoring methods, record sheets, and norm tables.

Unit 6 *Making Appropriate Use of Test Results and Providing Accurate Written and Oral Feedback to Clients and Candidates*

This unit stresses the interpersonal skills needed for face-to-face feedback as well as the oral and written communication skills required to convey technical information accurately in lay terms. It includes: use of appropriate norms and cut-offs; suitably cautious interpretations; standard errors; placing norm-based scores in appropriate contexts; describing scores clearly; reflecting confidence limits (including the effect of correlation between scale scores); relating test performance to person specification appropriately; computing composite test battery scores from weights provided; using appropriate and accurate language in describing tests and scales in lay terms; encouraging candidate participation in feedback sessions and their comments on the test(s) etc.; issues of how and to whom information should be presented; and clear guidance on the appropriate weight to attach to findings.

Unit 7 *Maintaining Security and Confidentiality of the Test Materials and the Test Data*

This covers the usual issues, including the Data Protection Act. Stress is laid on making rights and obligations clear to clients and candidates, e.g. information on how results will be used, who will have access to them, and how long they will be retained.

AIMS OF THE PROFESSIONAL NEWS SECTION

John Toplis

It is hoped to include the following in future issues:

- Appointments made; these will be "Top Appointments", such as University Chairs, or Head of Human Resources in major European organizations.
- Grants available; news of grants available from major European organizations will be welcome.
- Grants obtained.
- International conferences; as well as the dates of the conferences, closing dates for the submission of papers will be announced when available.
- News of networks; we hope that the newsletter will help with the formation and development of networks.
- Legal issues; the implications of European law in the areas of recruitment, employment and industrial relations is likely to be of particular interest to readers.
- Research collaboration; many individuals and groups will want to initiate comparative research studies across a number of European countries and perhaps outside the EEC as well—the professional news section will give researchers an opportunity to make contact with each other.
- Reports of both "confirmatory" and "unsuccessful" research findings.
- The comparison of alternative methodologies.

In addition I propose to collect contributions for a series of special features; each issue will contain at least one special feature, aimed at giving an up-to-date picture of professional practice and current issues.

I should be grateful if readers and contributors could help in the following ways:

1. Please let me have your views about possible regular/special features.
2. Please send contributions; please add your fax number to your contribution as well as other information such as your name, address and telephone number. If possible please send files in ASCII on IBM-compatible disks as well as hard copy—it could save me a great deal of time if you have written a lengthy article; I will, of course, return the disk.
3. Please forward copies of this section to anyone who might be interested, and encourage them to contribute.

I very much look forward to receiving your views as to how the Professional News Section might develop. Above all, I look forward to receiving your contributions.

National Correspondents

Finland

Kari Murto
Kaskik 2 as 13
40320 Jyväskylä
Finland

Germany

Dr. Conny Antoni
Fakultät für Psychologie
   und Sportwissenschaft
Universität Bielefeld
Postfach 100131
33501 Bielefeld
Germany

Greece

Dr. Aristotle Kantas
Applied Psychology Centre

Ariatotelous 96
10434 Athens
Greece

Portugal

Paulo M.C. Nunes de Abreu
ISEG
Rua Miguel Lupi, Gab. 414
1200 Lisboa, Portugal
Fax: +3511 396 64 07
Email: pna@baynes.iseg.utl.pt

United Kingdom

Wendy Fountain
The Assessment Consultancy
Training & Development Group
The Post Office
49 Featherstone Street
London EC1Y 8SY, UK

FORTHCOMING INTERNATIONAL CONFERENCES

**EIGHTH EUROPEAN CONGRESS ON
WORK AND ORGANIZATIONAL
PSYCHOLOGY**
2–5 APRIL 1997
VERONA, ITALY
Information:
EAWOP SECRETARIAT
Coosemansstraat 100
3010 Leuven
BELGIUM
Telefax/Phone: +32/16/25.78.15
Email: karel.dewitte@psy.kuleuven.ac.be

**XIII INTERNATIONAL SYMPOSIUM
ON NIGHT AND SHIFTWORK**
23–27 JUNE 1997
MAJVIK, FINLAND
Information:
Symposium on Night and Shiftwork
Symposium Secretariat, Suvi Lehtinen
Finnish Institute of Occupational Health
Topeliuksenkatu 41 a A
FIN-00250 Helsinki
FINLAND
Tel: 358-0-47 471
Fax: 358-0-474 7548
Email: leh@occuphealth.fi

**INTERNATIONAL ERGONOMICS
ASSOCIATION 13th TRIENNIAL
CONGRESS**
29 JUNE–4 JULY 1997
TAMPERE, FINLAND
Information:
Mr Markku Leppänen
Tampere University of Technology
P.O. Box 589
FIN-33101 Tampere, Finland
Tel: Int + 358-31-316 2581
Fax: Int + 358-31-316-2671
Email: mleppane@cc.tut.fi

**24th INTERNATIONAL CONGRESS
OF APPLIED PSYCHOLOGY**
9–14 AUGUST 1998
SAN FRANCISCO, USA
Information:
Congress Secretariat
APA Office of International Affairs
750 First Street, NE
Washington DC 20002, USA
Tel: +202-336-6024
Fax: +202-336-5956
Email: icap@apa.org

Aims and Scope

European Journal of Work and Organizational Psychology aims to bridge the gap between academics and practitioners by integrating European professional and academic responses to problems and issues which arise in practice.

From Volume 5 (1996) onwards, under the editorship of Dr Peter Herriot, each number of the Journal will address a specific issue which has been selected with an eye to the interests of practice rather than academia. Two guest editors will be appointed for each number, one a professional, the other an academic. These guest editors will invite contributions from prominent researchers and practitioners in that particular field.

Submission of Manuscripts

Submissions to *European Journal of Work and Organizational Psychology* are welcome from practitioners and academics. Submissions may take several forms; empirical research articles, reviews, case studies, descriptions and evaluations of instruments and systems, dialogues between academics and practitioners, intervention methods, and so on. If you wish to submit a contribution on any of the following topics, please write to the Editor at Psychology Press, 2 Park Square, Milton Park, Abingdon, Oxfordshire, OX14 4RN: team diversity and team functioning; training for new forms of leadership; performance improvement programmes in Europe; and power dynamics and resistance to change. You will receive names and addresses of the guest editors of the appropriate number of the Journal, along with some detailed instructions for authors concerning the appropriate layout of your article. The guest editors will review your manuscript in the usual manner and correspond with you thereafter.

Professional News

The Professional News section comprises regular items together with one or two special features. Regular items include appointments, news about grants, international conferences, news of networks, legal issues, and research collaboration. Special features are aimed at giving an up-to-date picture of professional practice and current issues.

All contributions for this section should be sent directly to the Professional News Editor, John Toplis, Management Development and Career Adviser, Training and Development Group, The Post Office, 49 Featherstone Street, London EC1Y 8SY, UK.

For Product Safety Concerns and Information please contact our EU
representative GPSR@taylorandfrancis.com Taylor & Francis Verlag GmbH,
Kaufingerstraße 24, 80331 München, Germany

Printed and bound by CPI Group (UK) Ltd, Croydon, CR0 4YY
08/05/2025
01864489-0005